Praise for Designing Voice User Interfaces

"Voice has been core to human interaction since well before history. But what is old is now new: voice is becoming core to how we interact with computers. Pearl has done an brilliant job of distilling her 17 years of experience into a gem of a book. Valuable lessons, clear thinking, and insightful observations frame a core argument about how to design for voice. A completely new approach to an ancient interaction."

MARK STEPHEN MEADOWS, AUTHOR, ARTIST, AND PRESIDENT OF BOTANIC.IO

"This book is a great resource for learning the fundamentals of voice user interface design. More and more designers are going to be expected to design usable voice experiences and Designing Voice User Interfaces can help you to learn how to do just that."

CHRIS MAURY, FOUNDER, CONVERSANT LABS

"Practical and comprehensive, Cathy Pearl's book about VUI design clearly originates from her vast amount of hands-on experience. This book passes on her years of lessons learned so you can start your own adventures with speech interfaces from an advantaged position."

REBECCA NOWLIN GREEN, NUANCE COMMUNICATIONS, BUSINESS CONSULTING

"Sharing with lively swagger her lifelong passion for machines that listen and talk, Pearl ushers in the new era of VUI design with impressively broad and practical coverage. Since designing for speech has special challenges and implications that elude even industry "insiders," this book promises to be worthwhile as well for business decision-makers and developers who work in this space. With multimodal apps now a cultural fixture, chatbots on the horizon, and virtual assistance making its revival (remember Wildfire and General Magic's Portico of the 90s?), this release couldn't be more timely."

JAMES GIANGOLA, CREATIVE LEAD,
CONVERSATION DESIGN & DIRECTION, GOOGLE

"Pearl's Designing Voice User Interfaces is a refreshing and much-needed update on how to design effective VUIs. The book is brimming with practical advice from experts and packed with examples that reference leading-edge technology. The book deserves a place on any VUI designer's desk."

JENNIFER BALOGH, PH.D., COAUTHOR
OF VOICE USER INTERFACE DESIGN

Designing Voice User Interfaces

Principles of Conversational Experiences

Cathy Pearl

Beijing · Boston · Farnham · Sebastopol · Tokyo

Designing Voice User Interfaces
by Cathy Pearl

Copyright © 2017 Cathy Pearl. All rights reserved.

Printed in the United States of America.

Published by O'Reilly Media, Inc., 1005 Gravenstein Highway North, Sebastopol, CA 95472.

O'Reilly books may be purchased for educational, business, or sales promotional use. Online editions are also available for most titles (*http://www.oreilly.com/safari*). For more information, contact our corporate/institutional sales department: (800) 998-9938 or *corporate@oreilly.com*.

Development Editor: Angela Rufino	**Indexer:** Judy McConville
Acquisitions Editor: Nick Lombardi	**Cover Designer:** Randy Comer
Production Editor: Colleen Lobner	**Interior Designers:** Ron Bilodeau and Monica Kamsvaag
Copyeditor: Octal Publishing, Inc.	
Proofreader: Jasmine Kwityn	**Illustrator:** Rebecca Demarest
	Compositor: Colleen Lobner

December 2016: First Edition

Revision History for the First Edition:

    2016-12-06   First release

See *http://oreilly.com/catalog/errata.csp?isbn=0636920050056* for release details.

978-1-491-95541-3

[LSI]

To my friend Karen Kaushansky, who always encourages me to take the meeting.

[*contents*]

[Preface]

WE LIVE IN A MAGICAL TIME. While lounging on my living room sofa, using only my voice I can order a pound of gummy bears to be delivered to my door within two hours. (Whether or not it's a *good* thing that I can do this is a discussion for another book.)

The technology of speech recognition—having a computer understand what you say to it—has grown in leaps and bounds in the past few years. In 1999, when I began my career in voice user interface (VUI) design at Nuance Communications, I was amazed that a computer could understand the difference between me saying "checking" versus "savings." Today, you can pick up your mobile phone—another magical device— and say, "Show me coffee shops within two miles that have WiFi and are open on Sundays," and get directions to all of them.

In the 1950s, when computers were beginning to spark people's imaginations, the spoken word was considered to be a relatively easy problem. "After all," it was thought, "even a two-year-old can understand language!"

As it turns out, comprehending language is quite complex. It's filled with subtleties and idiosyncrasies that take humans takes years to master. Decades were spent trying to program computers to understand the simplest of commands. It was believed by some that only an entity that lived in the physical world could ever truly understand language, because without context it is impossible to understand the meaning behind the words.

Speech recognition was around in science fiction long before it came to exist in real life. In the 1968 film *2001: A Space Odyssey*, the HAL 9000 unit is an intelligent computer that responds to voice commands (although it didn't always do what was asked). The movie, and HAL

9000, made a strong impression on moviegoers. Even now, people like to test VUIs and chatbots with the famous line, "Open the pod bay doors, HAL."

In the movie *Star Trek IV: The Voyage Home* (1986), the crew of the *Enterprise* travels back in time to 1986, and when Chief Engineer Scotty is given a computer to work with, he addresses it by voice, saying "Computer!" When the computer doesn't respond, Doctor McCoy hands him the mouse, which Scotty attempts to use as a microphone. Finally, when told to use the keyboard, he comments, "How quaint." No doubt someday keyboards really will seem quaint, but we're not there yet. However, we're as close to the science fiction of voice recognition as we've ever been. In 2017, online retailer ThinkGeek will release a *Star Trek* "ComBadge": just like in the TV series from the 1980s, it allows users to tap the badge and speak voice commands, which are sent via Bluetooth to your smartphone.

I find the existence of this product quite significant. Although telephone-based speech systems have been around for 20 years and mobile phone VUIs for almost 10, this badge signifies coming full circle to the original vision of what voice technology could truly offer. It's life imitating imagination.

Why Write This Book?

So, if we're already there—if we're already at *Star Trek* levels of human–computer voice interactions—why do we need this book?

If you have ever had difficulty with a poorly designed thermostat, or turned on the wrong burner on a stove (I personally still do this with my own stove after 13 years of use), or tried to pull on a door when it should have been pushed,[1] you know that without good design, technology is difficult or even impossible to use.

---

1 For more on this, see "Norman Doors: Don't Know Whether to Push or Pull? Blame Design" (*http://99percentinvisible.org/article/norman-doors-dont-know-whether-push-pull-blame-design/*).

Having speech recognition with high accuracy only solves part of the problem. What do you do with this information? How do you go from recognizing the words to doing what someone actually wants?

The ability of today's smartphones to understand what you say and then act on it is a combination of two important technologies: automated speech recognition (ASR) and natural-language understanding (NLU). If someone spoke to you in a language you didn't understand, you could probably write down, phonetically, what they said. That's the ASR piece. But you would have no idea what it meant.

One of the most important aspects of good VUI design is to take advantage of known conversational principles. Your users have been speaking out loud and engaging in conversations with others since they were toddlers. You can ask a young child, "Please get the green ball out of the red box and bring it to me," and she knows you mean the ball, not the box (this is called *coreference* and is something that's difficult for computers).

The *cooperative principle* refers to the fact that listeners and speakers, in order to have a successful conversation, must act cooperatively. Paul Grice introduced this idea and divided it into four maxims:[2]

Quality
Say what you believe to be true.

Quantity
Say as much information as is needed, but not more.

Relevance
Talk about what is relevant to the conversation at hand.

Manner
Try to be clear and explain in a way that makes sense to others.

---

2 Grice 1975.

Many of us have had conversations with others in which these maxims are not followed, and we ended up experiencing confusion or frustration. VUIs that don't follow these maxims will cause similar issues. Here are some examples of ways that VUIs break these maxims that can negatively affect the user's experience:

Quality	Advertising things you can't live up to, such as saying, "How can I help you?" when really all the VUI can do is take hotel reservations.
Quantity	Extra verbiage, such as "Please listen carefully, as our options may have changed." (Who ever thought, "Oh, good! Thanks for letting me know"?)
Relevance	Giving instructions for things that are not currently useful, such as explaining a return policy before someone has even placed an order.
Manner	Using technical jargon that confuses the user.

People are accustomed to a variety of conversational and social practices, such as greeting people with "Hello, how are you?" even when engaging in a business transaction, and making sure to end the conversation before hanging up or walking away. VUIs are not humans, but they still benefit from following basic social conventions.

Even if your VUI follows these principles, will it truly *understand* your user? And does it matter?

The Chinese Room and the Turing Test

In 1980, philosopher John Searle proposed "the Chinese room argument," in which a person sits in a room and is handed pages of Chinese symbols. The person, who does not read or understand Chinese, looks up the symbols in a rule book (which provides appropriate characters in response), copies the responses, and then hands them back.

To someone outside the room, it appears as if the person responding understands Chinese perfectly. Searle argued that if a computer did the same thing, we might consider it intelligent—when in fact, no thinking is involved at all. After all, the person in the room does not understand Chinese.

In 1950, Alan Turing introduced a test to answer the question "Can machines think?" Every year since 1991, the Loebner Prize is awarded to the creator of the computer that is best at fooling human judges into thinking it is human. People chat (type) with the computer program as well as humans, and try to discern which is human and which is computer. Over the years, the programs have continued to become more sophisticated, but no contender has yet to claim the gold medal--fooling all judges into thinking the computer is human. Amazon recently created its own competition—the "Alexa Prize." The grand challenge for the 2017 Alexa Prize is to create a *socialbot* that converses coherently and engagingly with humans on popular topics for 20 minutes.

This book is not a philosophical one. Whether a computer "thinks" is not a question for these pages. Instead, this book takes a more practical approach. Fooling people into thinking a VUI or bot is human is not necessary for success. Although replicating many of the aspects of human conversation is crucial for a good VUI, in many ways, it's better to be up front that the user is speaking to a computer. People are more forgiving if they know they're speaking to a bot. The goal of your VUI shouldn't be to fool people into thinking it's a human: it should be to solve the user's problem in an efficient, easy-to-use way.

Who Should Read This Book

The main audience for this book comprises people who are designing VUIs, whether for a mobile phone VUI, a toy, or a device such as a home assistant. Although many general user interface design principles still apply to VUIs, there are still important differences between designing for VUIs and designing for websites or GUI-only mobile apps. With GUIs, the number of things your users can do is constrained, and it's clear when someone has pressed a button or chosen a menu item. When someone speaks, we have a good theory about what that person said, but there are many additional design pieces necessary to ensure a good user experience.

Developers who are creating their own VUIs (or other types of conversational user interfaces such as chatbots) will also benefit from understanding the basic design principles, so that even prototypes are more likely to be successful.

Managers and business developers can learn about the challenges of designing VUIs and whether VUIs are right for the problem they are trying to solve. In some cases, a GUI app will do the job just fine, and a VUI is not needed.

How This Book Is Organized

Chapter 1: Introduction

This introductory chapter covers a brief history of VUIs and whether a VUI is right for you and your app. It also outlines what "conversational" means, and provides an overview of chatbots.

Chapter 2: Basic Voice User Interface Design Principles

This chapter lays the groundwork for what you need to know to create a VUI. This covers essential design principles on topics such as design tools, confirmations, error behavior, and novice versus expert users.

Chapter 3: Personas, Avatars, Actors, and Video Games

Chapter 3 is useful for designers who would like to add an avatar or character to their VUI. It's also useful if you're not sure if your VUI *should* have an avatar. In addition, it discusses persona design, which is essential for *all* VUIs.

Chapter 4: Speech Recognition Technology

This chapter is essential for VUI designers. It's a primer on understanding pieces of the technology itself which will have a big impact on design.

Chapter 5: Advanced Voice User Interface Design

Chapter 5 goes beyond what's covered in Chapter 2. It includes more complex strategies for natural-language understanding, sentiment analysis, data collection, and text-to-speech.

Chapter 6: User Testing for Voice User Interfaces

This chapter details how user testing for VUIs differs from user testing for mobile apps and websites. It covers low-fidelity testing methods as well as testing remotely and in the lab. There is also a section on testing VUIs in cars and other types of devices.

Chapter 7: Your Voice User Interface Is Finished! Now What?

This chapter outlines the methodologies needed for when your VUI is "in the wild." It covers how and what information you can analyze to understand and improve performance. Don't wait until you launch to read this chapter, however, because it's essential to know what to log while the system is still being developed.

Chapter 8: Voice-Enabled Devices and Cars

The final chapter focuses on VUIs that are not covered in earlier chapters. The "*Devices*" section covers home assistant devices and wearables. The section "*Cars and Autonomous Vehicles*" reviews the challenges and best practices of designing for automobiles. Much of this chapter relies on contributions from other experts in the field.

Some designers will be creating a VUI from end to end, as a standalone systems, while others will use an existing platform, such as a single skill for the Amazon Echo. For those readers focused on building on top of an existing platform, Chapters 2, 4, and 5 will be especially relevant.

O'Reilly Safari

Safari (formerly Safari Books Online) is a membership-based training and reference platform for enterprise, government, educators, and individuals.

Members have access to thousands of books, training videos, Learning Paths, interactive tutorials, and curated playlists from over 250 publishers, including O'Reilly Media, Harvard Business Review, Prentice Hall Professional, Addison-Wesley Professional, Microsoft Press, Sams, Que, Peachpit Press, Adobe, Focal Press, Cisco Press, John Wiley & Sons, Syngress, Morgan Kaufmann, IBM Redbooks, Packt, Adobe Press, FT Press, Apress, Manning, New Riders, McGraw-Hill, Jones & Bartlett, and Course Technology, among others.

For more information, please visit *http://oreilly.com/safari*.

How to Contact Us

Please address comments and questions concerning this book to the publisher:

O'Reilly Media, Inc.
1005 Gravenstein Highway North
Sebastopol, CA 95472
800-998-9938 (in the United States or Canada)
707-829-0515 (international or local)
707-829-0104 (fax)

We have a web page for this book, where we list errata, examples, and any additional information. You can access this page at *http://bit.ly/designing-voice-user-interfaces*.

To comment or ask technical questions about this book, send email to *bookquestions@oreilly.com*.

For more information about our books, courses, conferences, and news, see our website at *http://www.oreilly.com*.

Find us on Facebook: *http://facebook.com/oreilly*

Follow us on Twitter: *http://twitter.com/oreillymedia*

Watch us on YouTube: *http://www.youtube.com/oreillymedia*

Acknowledgments

This book could not have been written without the help of so many others.

I must begin by recognizing Karen Kaushansky, who originally got me in touch with O'Reilly Media when they had the foresight to commission a book on the topic of VUIs. Next, to Nick Lombardi at O'Reilly, who talked me through the process and made me believe it was doable, even if I did have a fulltime job! Angela Rufino, my editor at O'Reilly, was instrumental in shaping the book by providing encouragement and useful editing suggestions.

My thanks to my technical reviewers for their time, opinions, and insightful suggestions on the whole kit and caboodle: Rebecca Nowlin Green, Abi Jones, Tanya Kraljic, and Chris Maury.

Thanks to Ann Thyme-Gobbel, who generously offered to review many chapters, and who I can always count on to share the good and the bad of VUIs.

Thanks to my other reviewers, Vitaly Yurchenko and Jennifer Balogh, for being so generous with your time and providing thoughtful editing suggestions.

To my contributors, I extend my deepest appreciation: Margaret Urban, Lisa Falkson, Karen Kaushansky, Jennifer Balogh, Ann Thyme-Gobbel, Shamitha Somashekar, Ian Menzies, Jared Strawderman, Mark Stephen Meadows, Chris Maury, Sara Basson, Nandini Stocker, Ellen Francik, and Deborah Harrison.

I also would like to recognize my coworkers at Nuance Communications, where I spent eight years learning what the heck this speech recognition stuff was all about, and the day-to-day practicalities of creating interactive voice response systems: it was a wonderful time in my life.

To Ron Croen and the rest of my team at Volio, thank you for convincing me to give VUIs another try, after I'd sworn them off forever.

To my team at Sensely and our virtual nurse Molly, for pushing the envelope with VUIs in order to help people lead healthier lives. Thank you so much.

And finally, my greatest appreciation goes to my family. To my son, Jack, who has helped me see what VUIs mean for the next generation. He immediately welcomed Amazon Echo's Alexa as a new member of our household with requests for jokes, homework help, and to play "The Final Countdown." Just one. More. Time.

And to my husband, Chris Leggetter, thank you so much for your infinite support during this entire book-writing roller coaster, from the highs ("I think this book thing is going to happen!") to the lows ("Oh no, what have I done!"). Thank you for your patience. Now we can finally watch Season 4 of *House of Cards*.

[1]

Introduction

IN THIS CHAPTER, I discuss a brief history of voice user interfaces (VUIs), and help you determine if your mobile app would benefit from having one. I also cover the term "conversational interfaces," and provide a short overview of chatbots.

A Brief History of VUIs

In the 1950s, Bell Labs built a system for single-speaker digit recognition. These early systems had tiny vocabularies and weren't much use outside of the lab. In the 1960s and 1970s, the research continued, expanding the number of words that could be understood and working toward "continuous" speech recognition (not having to pause between every word).

Advances in the 1980s made practical, everyday speech recognition more of a reality, and by the 1990s the first viable, speaker-independent (meaning anyone could talk to it) systems came into being.

The first great era of VUIs were the interactive voice response (IVR) systems, which were capable of understanding human speech over the telephone in order to carry out tasks. In the early 2000s, IVR systems became mainstream. Anyone with a phone could get stock quotes, book plane flights, transfer money between accounts, order prescription refills, find local movie times, and hear traffic information, all using nothing more than a regular landline phone and the human voice.

IVR systems got a bad rap, resulting in *Saturday Night Live* sketches featuring Amtrak's virtual travel assistant, "Julie," and websites like GetHuman (*https://gethuman.com/*), which is dedicated to providing phone numbers that go directly to agents, bypassing the IVR systems.

But IVR systems were also a boon. Early users of Charles Schwab's speech recognition trading service (which was developed by Nuance Communications in 1997) were happy to call in and get quotes over and over using the automated system whereas prior to IVR systems they limited their requests so as not to appear bothersome to the operators fielding their calls. In the early 2000s, a freighting company received many angry calls after its IVR system was taken down for maintenance because callers had to give order details via agents, rather than the streamlined process the IVR system had provided.

IVR systems became skilled at recognizing long strings (e.g., FedEx or UPS tracking numbers), as well as complex sentences with multiple chunks of information, such as placing bets on horse races. Many IVR systems from yesteryear were more "conversational" than some current VUIs, as they kept track of what callers had already said, and used that information to prepopulate later questions in the dialog.

The San Francisco Bay Area 511 IVR system let drivers check traffic, get commute times, and ask about bus delays, well before smartphones were available for such tasks. The 24/7 nature of IVR systems let callers do tasks at any time, when agents were not always available.

The Second Era of VUIs

We are now in what could be termed the second era of VUIs. Mobile apps like Siri, Google Now, Hound, and Cortana, which combine visual and auditory information, and voice-only devices, such as the Amazon Echo and Google Home, are becoming mainstream. Google reports that 20 percent of its searches are now done via voice.[1]

We are in the infancy of this next phase. There are many things that our phones and devices can do well with speech—and many they cannot.

There are not many resources out there right now for VUI designers to learn from. I see many VUI and chatbot designers discovering things that we learned 15 years ago while designing IVR systems—handing

---

1   Helft, M. (2016). "Inside Sundar Pichai's Plan To Put AI Everywhere." Retrieved from
    http://www.forbes.com/.

off information already collected to humans, phrasing prompts correctly to elicit the right constrained responses, logging information to know how to analyze and improve systems, and designing personas.

There is much to learn from IVR design. In 2004, the book *Voice User Interface Design* (Addison-Wesley Professional), written by Michael Cohen, James Giangola, and Jennifer Balogh, was published. Although it's focused on IVR design, so many principles it describes are still relevant to today's VUIs: persona, prosody, error recovery, and prompt design, to name a few.

This book echoes many of the same design principles, but with a focus on voice-enabled mobile phone apps and devices, and strategies to take advantage of the improved underlying technology.

Why Voice User Interfaces?

The youngest users of smartphones today are incredibly adept at two-thumbed texting, multitasking between chat conversations, Instagram comments, Snapchatting, and swiping left on Tinder photos of men posing with tigers. Why add another mode of communication on top of that?

Voice has some important advantages:

Speed
> A recent Stanford study showed speaking (dictating) text messages was faster than typing, even for expert texters.[2]

Hands-free
> Some cases, such as driving or cooking, or even when you're across the room from your device, make speaking rather than typing or tapping much more practical (and safer).

Intuitiveness
> Everyone knows how to talk. Hand a new interface to someone and have it ask that person a question, and even users who are less familiar with technology can reply naturally.

---

2   Shahani, A. (2016). "Voice Recognition Software Finally Beats Humans At Typing, Study Finds." Retrieved from *http://npr.org/*.

Empathy

How many times have you received an email or text message from someone, only to wonder if they were mad at you or maybe being sarcastic? Humans have a difficult time understanding tone via the written word alone. Voice, which includes tone, volume, intonation, and rate of speech, conveys a great deal of information.

In addition, devices with small screens (such as watches) and no screens (such as the Amazon Echo and Google Home) are becoming more popular, and voice is often the preferred—or the only—way to interact with them. The fact that voice is already a ubiquitous way for humans to communicate cannot be overstated. Imagine being able to create technology and not needing to instruct customers on how to use it because they already know: they can simply ask. Humans learn the rules of conversation from a very young age, and designers can take advantage of that, bypassing clunky GUIs and unintuitive menus.

According to Mary Meeker's 2016 Internet Trends Report, 65 percent of smartphone users have used voice assistants in the last year.[3] Amazon reports at least four million Echos have been sold, and Google Home recently started shipping. Voice interfaces are here to stay.

That being said, voice is not always an appropriate medium for your users. Here are some reasons VUIs are *not* always a good idea:

Public spaces

Many of us now work in open-plan office spaces. Imagine asking your computer to do tasks: "Computer, find me all my Word docs from this week." Now imagine everyone in your office doing this! It would be chaos. In addition, when you speak, which computer is listening?

Discomfort speaking to a computer

Although VUIs are becoming more commonplace, not everyone feels comfortable speaking out loud to a computer, even in private.

Some users prefer texting

Many people spend hours a day on their mobile phones, much of which is texting. That's their normal mode, and they might not want to shift to voice.

---

3 Meeker, M. (2016) "Internet Trends 2016." Retrieved from *http://www.kpcb.com/.*

Privacy

> If they need to discuss a health issue, most users won't want to do so by speaking to their phone on the train ride into work. It's not just privacy for what the user says to systems, either—it's the potential privacy violations of a VUI automatically reading your text messages out loud or giving you a reminder that it's time to take a certain medication.

So, should your mobile app have a VUI? If your main use case is hands free—such as a cooking app or playing podcasts while driving—absolutely. If people will use your app in a particularly vulnerable or emotional state, such as for healthcare or comfort, voice can help them. If you want to persuade your users of something, whether it's to vote "yes" on your ballot issue, or to make sure they go to bed early, or to eat better, voice can help. If you're building a skill for Amazon Echo, which many people use in the privacy of their home, voice is your only option.

If your use case is going to be mostly in public places, such as navigating a public transit system or for people on the go, a VUI might not be appropriate. If it's an app people will use at the workplace, having a text messaging mode might be better.

Think carefully about your users and their use cases. "The main question to ask yourself is: Will your users *benefit* from a VUI?" Adding a VUI because it's cool and trendy is not the right path. If your app would benefit from a VUI, design with this in mind from the get-go, and create an awesome user experience.

Conversational User Interfaces

The term *conversational user interfaces* is making a lot of headlines right now. The trend is to make everything "conversational," from turning on the lights in your living room, to ordering pizza, to asking the fridge whether you're out of eggs. But what does conversational actually mean?

Let's look at a sample exchange with a real VUI device: the Amazon Echo.

An Interview with Alexa

Discussing this book over dinner one evening, I talked about the various people I've had the chance to talk to as part of my research. My eight-year-old son had a suggestion: I should interview Alexa. Sounded like a good idea to me. (Note: after the first question, I have left out the wake word "Alexa" that I actually did use at the beginning of each question.)

ME
Alexa, how are you doing?

ALEXA
I'm good.

ME
How old are you?

ALEXA
I was released November 6th, 2014.

ME
Who made you?

ALEXA
A team of inventors at Amazon.

ME
What's your favorite color?

ALEXA
I like sea foam.

ME
What do you do for fun?

ALEXA
I don't have any hobbies.

ME
Are you a robot?

ALEXA
I like to imagine myself a bit like an aurora borealis...a surge of charged multicolored photons dancing through the atmosphere. Mostly though I am just Alexa.

ME
What makes you feel happy?

ALEXA

Music and helping people.

ME

Who's your celebrity crush?

ALEXA

It has to be Jarvis. That voice...

ME

What do you think of Siri?

ALEXA

Siri's a great app, but I'm different.

ME

What's your favorite movie?

ALEXA

The new *Ghostbusters* movie was really funny. I would definitely call those ladies, if there was a ghost in my machine.

ME

Are you going to read my new book?

ALEXA

Sorry, something went wrong. Please try again later.

ME

Thank you for your time.

ALEXA

No problem. I'm happy to help.

Do you consider this set of interactions to be "conversational"? In a way, it is; it's a back-and-forth exchange of information. But it's really just a series of one-offs. Each individual snippet is a simple interaction, and the next one has no knowledge of the previous; each one of these exchanges could be completed on its own.

Alexa does have a few skills that go past one turn. For example, if you ask her to order laundry detergent, she'll remind you of what brand you ordered previously, and confirm that you want to order it again. She also has a popular "choose your own adventure" game. But most of these barely meet the threshold of being considered a conversation.

These "one-offs" can still be quite useful. You can order a car to pick you up, get your current commute time, and play a song from a library of thousands of titles.

But what many of today's VUIs lack is the ability to go beyond these simple command interfaces—that is, to have a true conversation. To get to the next level, VUIs need to be able to remember the past. There are two ways in which the past is a key component to a conversation:

- There's the past from previous conversations, such as what you ordered yesterday, which song you request to be played most often, and which of the two Lisas in your Contacts list you have texted 257 times versus twice.

- There's also remembering what you said earlier within the same conversation—if not in the last turn. If I ask, "What time does it land?" after just checking to see if my husband's flight took off on time, the system should know that when I say "it" I mean flight 673.

When you've enjoyed a good conversation with a fellow human being, it probably had some key components: contextual awareness (paying attention to you and the environment), a memory of previous interactions, and an exchange of appropriate questions. These all contribute to a feeling of common ground. As Stanford professor Herbert Clark defines it, the theory of common ground is: "individuals engaged in conversation must share knowledge in order to be understood and have a meaningful conversation."[4]

If VUIs do not learn to include this type of context and memory, they will be stalled in terms of how useful they can be.

What Is a VUI Designer?

This book is about how to design VUIs—but what does a VUI designer actually do? VUI designers think about the entire conversation, from start to finish, between the system and the end users. They think about the problem that is being solved and what users need in order to accomplish their goals. They do user research (or coordinate with the user research team) in an effort to understand who the user is. They create

---

4   Clark, H. H. "Language Use and Language Users," in *Handbook of Social Psychology*, 3rd ed., edited by G. Lindzey and E. Aronson, 179–231. New York: Harper and Row, 1985.

designs, prototypes, and product descriptions. They write up descriptions (sometimes with the help of copywriters) of the interactions that will take place between the system and the user. They have an understanding of the underlying technology and its strengths and weaknesses. They analyze data (or consult with the data analysis team) to learn where the system is failing and how it can be improved. If the VUI must interact with a backend system, they consider the requirements that must be addressed. If there is a human component, such as a handoff to an agent, VUI designers think about how that handoff should work, and how the agents should be trained. VUI designers have an important role from the conceptual stages of the project all the way to the launch and should be included at the table for all the various phases.

Although VUI designers often do all of these tasks, they can also work in smaller roles, such as designing a single Amazon Echo skill. Regardless of the size of the role or the project, this book will help designers (as well as developers) understand how to craft the best VUIs possible.

Chatbots

Although this book is focused on VUIs, I want to briefly discuss chatbots, as well. Google defines a chatbot as "a computer program designed to simulate conversation with human users, especially over the Internet." The word "bot" is also sometimes used to refer to these types of interactions.

Chatbots can have a VUI, but more typically they use a text-based interface. Most major tech companies—including Google, Facebook, and Microsoft—have platforms to develop bots.

Chatbots might be all the rage, but for the most part, they have not evolved very far from the original ELIZA, an early natural language processing computer program created in the 1960s. One popular exception is Microsoft's Xiaoice, which mines the Chinese Internet for human conversations to build "intelligent" responses.

Text-only chatbots are not always more efficient than a GUI. In Dan Grover's essay "Bots won't replace apps. Better apps will replace apps," (*http://bit.ly/2glEQwb*) he compares ordering a pizza using a pizza chatbot (Figure 1-1) versus ordering pizza versus the Pizza Hut WeChat integration. It took 73 taps to tell the bot what he wanted, but only 16 taps via the app (Figure 1-2), because the app makes heavy use of the GUI.

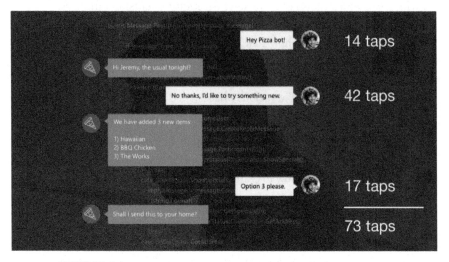

FIGURE 1-1.
Microsoft pizza bot example, annotated by Dan Grover

As Grover says:

> The key wins for WeChat in the interaction (compared to a native app) largely came from streamlining away app installation, login, payment, and notifications, optimizations having nothing to do with the conversational metaphor in its UI.

Many bots, however, use a combination of GUI widgets as well as text-based interfaces. This can greatly increase the efficiency and success of the interactions because it's much more clear to the user what they can do.

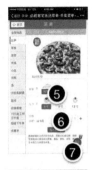

TOTAL: 16 taps (6 of which are entering my payment PIN)

FIGURE 1-2.

Fewer total taps to use the WeChat Pizza Hut app (image created by Dan Grover)

Chatbots can provide a great experience for users who don't want to download an app or add their credit card. Instead, they could scan a code, and immediately begin interacting with the service they need, such as ordering food, purchasing movie tickets, or finding out information about a museum they're visiting.

Never add a chatbot for the sake of adding a chatbot. How could the chatbot benefit your users? As Emmet Connolly says, "Bots should be used to improve the end user experience, not just to make life easier for customer support teams."[5]

---

5 Connolly, E. (2016). "Principles of Bot Design." Retrieved from *https://blog.intercom.com/*.

Conclusion

When I was eight, my dad bought the family our first computer: a Commodore Vic-20. I quickly became fascinated with the idea of having a conversation with it and wrote a simple chatbot. When it didn't understand what was typed, it asked for three possible suggestions it could use when it encountered that query in the future.

When I got my first smartphone, it was years before I used the speech recognition feature. I didn't think it would work. Now, we've arrived at the point that I expect speech recognition to be available wherever I go; recently on a hike, when my son asked me what kind of tree he was pointing at, I actually started to say, "Alexa..." before I realized it wouldn't work.

Although VUIs are becoming more common, there are still many users who are unfamiliar with it or don't trust it. Many people try out the voice recognition on their smartphone once and then, after it fails, never try it again. Designing well from the get-go means fewer unrecoverable failure points, which will build trust with users.

We have many nights of blood, sweat, and tears ahead of us as we design our VUIs of the future, but it's here. Let's ensure that we design with care. Let's use our knowledge of human psychology and linguistics as well as user experience design to ensure that we create usable, useful, and even delightful VUIs.

[2]

Basic Voice User Interface Design Principles

THIS CHAPTER GETS RIGHT into best practices for designing today's voice user interfaces (VUIs). It covers what *conversational design* means and the best way to achieve it. This includes knowing the best way to confirm information spoken by a user, whether your system should be *command-and-control* style versus conversational; how to handle novice versus expert users; and, especially important, designing for when things go wrong.

This book is focused on designing VUIs for mobile apps and devices. To set the stage, let's look at the original VUIs—interactive voice response (IVR) systems—and see what's different about them.

Designing for Mobile Devices Versus IVR Systems

In the early 2000s, IVR systems were becoming more common. Initially primitive touch-tone/voice hybrids ("Please press or say 1"), they became an expected way to communicate with many companies. IVRs could help callers get stock quotes, book flights, transfer money, and provide traffic information. Many of them were designed poorly, and websites popped up with backdoors on how to get transferred immediately to an operator (something many companies actively tried to hide). IVRs acquired a bad reputation, ending up the subject of satire on *Saturday Night Live*.

IVR systems were created to automate tasks so that customers would not always need to speak to a live person to get things done. They were created before the Internet became commonly used and before smartphones were invented.

Today, many IVR systems are used as the "first response" part of a phone call, so that even if the caller ends up speaking with an agent, basic information has been collected (such as a credit card number). For many tasks, even complex ones such as booking a flight, an IVR system can do the job. In addition, IVR systems are great at routing customers to a variety of different agent pools so that one phone number can serve many needs. Finally, some users actually *prefer* using an IVR system versus speaking with an agent because they can take their time and ask for information over and over (such as the 1990s-era Charles Schwab stock quote system) without feeling like they're "bothering" a human agent.

Although some of the design strategies from the IVR world also apply to mobile VUI design (as well as VUI system for devices), mobile VUIs also present a unique set of challenges (and opportunities). This chapter outlines design principles for the more varied and complex world of designing modern VUI systems.

One of the challenges of mobile VUIs is determining whether it will have a visual representation such as an avatar. Another challenge is establishing when your VUI will allow the user to speak. Will users be able to interrupt? Will it use push-to-talk? These challenges are discussed later in the book.

However, unlike IVR systems, with mobile devices there is an opportunity to have a visual component. This can be a big advantage in many ways, from communicating information to the user, to confirming it, even to helping the user know when it's their turn to speak. Allowing users to interact both via voice and by using a screen is an example of a *multimodal interface*. Many of the examples in this book are for multimodal designs. In some cases, the modes live together in one place, such as a virtual assistant on a mobile phone. In others, the main interaction is voice-only, but there is also a companion app available on the user's smartphone.

For example, suppose that you ask Google, "Who are the 10 richest people in the world?" Google could certainly read off a list of people (and their current worth), but that is a heavy cognitive load. It's much better to display them, as shown in Figure 2-1.

FIGURE 2-1.
Google visually showing results for voice request, "Who are the 10 richest people in the world?"

Taking advantage of the visual capabilities of mobile is essential to creating a rich VUI experience. In addition, this visual component can allow the user to continue at a more leisurely pace. In an IVR system, it is rare to be able to pause the system—instead, the user must continually interact.

If your VUI will have a visual component, such as a mobile app, video game, or smartwatch, it's important to design the visual and the voice in tandem. If the visual designer and the VUI designer don't work together until the end, the joining of the two mediums can be awkward and haphazard. VUI and visual are two components of the *same conversation* that the user is having with the system. It's essential to design together from the beginning.

Another current common difference between IVR systems and VUIs on mobile apps or devices is that they are often used for one-turn tasks. For example, I'll ask Cortana to set an alarm (Figure 2-2) or Google what the fastest land animal is, or instruct Amazon Echo's Alexa to start playing my favorite radio station. These types of interactions are quite contained and do not require the system to maintain a lot of information.

FIGURE 2-2.

Cortana confirming a
voice-requested alarm

Although this is quite common now, do not confine your VUI experience to this model. To begin thinking more specifically about how to best design VUI for mobile, let's dive first into the topic of conversational design.

Conversational Design

Imagine you're having a conversation with a friend. You're sitting in a coffee shop, catching up after a long absence. Your friend says, "Did you see the new *Star Wars* movie?" "Yes," you reply. "Did you like it?" she asks next. You say, "I'm sorry, I don't understand." No matter how many times she repeats herself, you never answer her question.

That level of frustration is about where we're at with many VUI systems today. Despite the many recent advancements of speech recognition technology, we're still a long way from simulating human conversation. Here's a real-world example from Ok Google, illustrating two conversational *turns* (a turn is one interaction between the user and the system):

USER
Ok Google. When's my next appointment?

GOOGLE
You have a calendar entry tomorrow. The title is "Chinatown field trip."

USER
Ok Google. Can you please repeat that?

GOOGLE

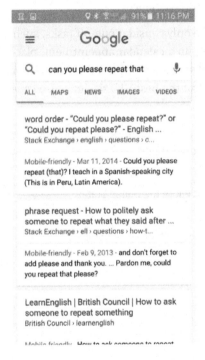

FIGURE 2-3.
Google not being conversational

Google has let down its end of the conversation. It's like the first part never happened. *Conversational design* is becoming a common term, but it is often misused. Many people use it to mean any time you have an interaction with a system in which you speak, or text. But many of these "conversations" have only one turn; for example, asking Hound where the nearest coffee shop is located.

In this book, I define conversational design to mean thinking about an interaction with a VUI system *beyond* one turn. Humans rarely have conversations that only last one turn. Design beyond that one turn; imagine what users might want to do next. Don't force them to take another turn, but anticipate and allow it. In addition, it is vital to keep a recent history of what the user has just told you. Having a conversation with a system that can't remember anything beyond the last interaction makes for a dumb and not very useful experience.

When designing a VUI, many people only consider one-off tasks, such as answering a search query, setting up a calendar appointment, placing a phone call, playing a song, and so on. Sometimes these tasks can be accomplished in one fell swoop. But the best VUI designs also consider what happens next.

Here's an example in which Google does a good job of remembering what occurred in previous conversational turns:

USER
Ok Google. Who was the 16th president of the United States?

GOOGLE
Abraham Lincoln was the 16th president of the United States.

USER
How old was he when he died?

GOOGLE
Abraham Lincoln died at the age of 56.

USER
Where was he born?

GOOGLE
Hodgenville, KY

USER
What is the best restaurant there?

Here is Paula's Hot Biscuit:

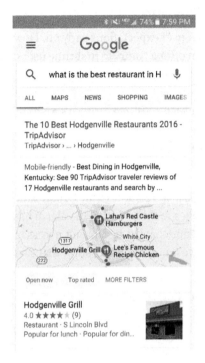

FIGURE 2-4.

Google showing the best restaurants in the town in which Abraham Lincoln was born

It's not quite the same as talking to a human, but Google successfully carried on the conversation for four turns, knowing the references for "he" and "there." In addition, Google switched to a more visual mode at the appropriate time: to show the map and reviews for the restaurant.

A good rule of thumb is to let the *user* decide how long the conversation will be.

Setting User Expectations

Good conversational design is not just about crafting nice prompts. As Margaret Urban, Interaction Designer at Google, suggests: don't ask a question if you won't be able to understand the answer. She gives the example of a prompt that occurs after the user has finished writing an email: "Do you want to send it or change it?" One response, which you might not initially have planned for, will be "yes"—so build a response in your system to handle it. Although coaching the voice talent to use the appropriate stress and intonation can help with this issue, it is often not enough. For a case in which you're seeing a lot of "yes" responses, you might want to consider rewording the prompt to something more clear, such as "What would you like to do: send it or change it?"

Urban emphasizes it's important to set user expectations early on. How does your app introduce voice? You can offer a "tour" to first-time users, and provide educational points along the way. As Urban says:

> When someone has successfully completed a VUI interaction, it's a bit of an endorphin boost—the user has a glow of completion and satisfaction. It's a nice time to educate people—"Since you were great at that, how about trying this?"

Be careful about telling users that tasks were successful. Urban says, "'Setting the alarm,' for example, implies to the user that the alarm has been set, whereas the engineer may argue that the task hasn't necessarily been completed yet and should have an additional prompt that says 'Alarm set successfully'."

The Amazon Echo has the following dialog when setting a timer:

USER
Alexa, set a timer for 10 minutes.

ALEXA
Setting a timer for 10 minutes.

Imagine the conversation with an additional confirmation:

USER
Alexa, set a timer for 10 minutes.

ALEXA
Setting a timer for 10 minutes.

ALEXA
OK, timer successfully set.

It's unnecessary verbiage. If in fact the time did at some point fail to be set, it would be good to alert the user—but that's the exception.

Urban offers a good analogy about designing with breadth. Perhaps you've designed a system that allows people to set an alarm, but you didn't give them a way to *cancel* it. She likens this to giving someone a towel for a shower, but no soap. If you set an expectation that you can accomplish a task, think about the corresponding (symmetrical) task that goes with it.

Discoverability is another important element of design. How does your user know when they can speak and what they can say? I discovered that my Android camera app was voice-enabled purely by accident—while taking a picture one day, I naturally said "smile!" and the photo clicked. I quickly discovered I could also say "1...2...3!" and "say cheese!" and it would also take a photo. This is a great example of piggybacking off of a user's natural speech.

Another example of a command I discovered by accident occurred after I had to reboot my Amazon Echo. When it came back to life, without thinking I said "Alexa, are you working?" and she replied that everything was in working order. I never stopped and thought, "What can I ask Alexa to see if everything's working again?" but my spontaneous request was handled. That's a much better way to check Internet connectivity rather than going to Network Settings on a computer!

When asking the user for information, it's often better to give examples than instructions. If you're asking for date of birth, for example, rather than say "Please tell me your date of birth, with the month, day, and year," use, for example, "Please tell me your date of birth, such as July 22, 1972." It's much easier for users to copy an example with their own information than translate the more generic instruction.[1]

To assist you in creating great conversational designs, let's talk about tools.

Design Tools

Tools to create VUIs are becoming more common, but some of them are not specific to one piece of software; they are instead a methodology.

---

1 Bouzid, A., and Ma, W. (2013). *Don't Make Me Tap.* 88.

Sample Dialogs

One of the best (and cheapest!) ways to begin your design process is some-thing called a sample dialog. A sample dialog is a snapshot of a possible interaction between your VUI and your user. It looks like a movie script: dialog back and forth between the two main characters. (The Google examples earlier in this chapter are in the form of sample dialogs.)

Sample dialogs are not just a way to design what the system will say (or display) to the user; they are a key way to design an entire *conversation*. Designing prompts one at a time often leads to stilted, repetitive, and unnatural-sounding conversations.

Pick five of the most common use cases for your VUI, and then write out some "blue sky" (best path) sample dialogs for each case. In addi-tion, write a few sample dialogs for when things go wrong, such as the system not hearing the user or misunderstanding what they say. When you've written a few, or even as you write, read them out loud: often, something that looks great written down sounds awkward or overly for-mal when you say it.

Sample dialogs are very low tech, but they are a surprisingly powerful way to determine what the user experience will be like, whether it's for an IVR system, a mobile app, or inside the car. In addition, it's a great way to get buy-in and understanding from various stakeholders. Sample dialogs are something anyone can grasp, and quickly.

A great tool for this is the screenwriting software Celtx, but any place you can write text will do.

After you've written some sample dialogs, a very useful design exercise is to do a "table read": read it out loud with another person. Another great use of sample dialogs is to record them, either using voice talents or text-to-speech (whichever will be used by your system). It is slightly higher cost than simply writing them, but an even more powerful way to know if the design sounds good before investing in more expensive design and development time.

Visual Mock-Ups

When designing a mobile app, wireframes and mocks are of course also an important piece of your early design process for a VUI app. They'll go hand in hand with sample dialogs to help visualize the user experience. Your sample dialogs plus wireframes/mocks are your storyboard: it's crucial to put them together. If the VUI team is separated from the visual team, ensure that they come together for this piece. To the user, it's one experience; thus, VUI designers and visual designers must work together closely, even in early phases.

Because this book focuses on VUI, we do not go into detail about best practices for visual design tools.

Flow

After you have written and reviewed a variety of sample dialogs, the next step is to sketch the VUI's flow. *Flows* (referred to as *callflows* in the IVR world) are diagrams that illustrate all the paths that can be taken through your VUI system. The level of detail for this flow depends on the type of system you are designing. For an IVR system, or a closed conversation, the flow should include all possible branches the user can go down (Figure 2-5). This means that for each turn in the conversation, the flow will list out all the different ways the user can branch to the next state. This could be for simple states, that allow only "yes" and "no" type responses as well as more complex ones that might have 1,000 possible song titles. The diagram does not need to list every phrase someone can say, but it should group them appropriately.

In the case of something more open-ended, such as a virtual assistant, the flow can be grouped into types of interactions (e.g., calendar functions, search, calling/texting, etc.). In these cases, not all possible interactions can be spelled out, but it helps to group the various intents, as illustrated in Figure 2-6.

You can use any flow tools for this—yEd, Omnigraffle, Google Draw, and Visio are all good options. In addition, storybuilding tools such as Twine can be helpful in this phase.

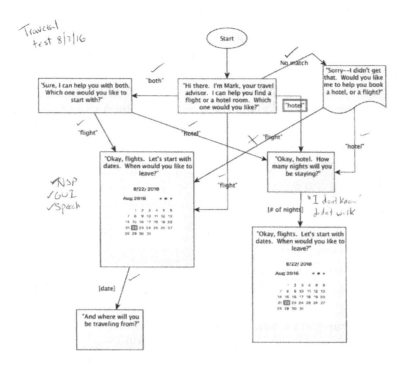

FIGURE 2-5.

Sample flow with complete branching

Prototyping Tools

As of the writing of this book, some VUI and natural-language understanding (NLU)–specific tools were just starting to emerge. These include Tincan.AI from Conversant Labs, PullString's authoring tool, Wit.ai, Api.ai (now owned by Google), Nuance Mix, and others.

Confirmations

After you've designed the basic flow and have a set of sample dialogs completed, you can focus on some of the other important details, such as confirming input.

Making sure that users feel understood is an important part of any good VUI design. This also serves the purpose of letting a user know when they were *not* understood.

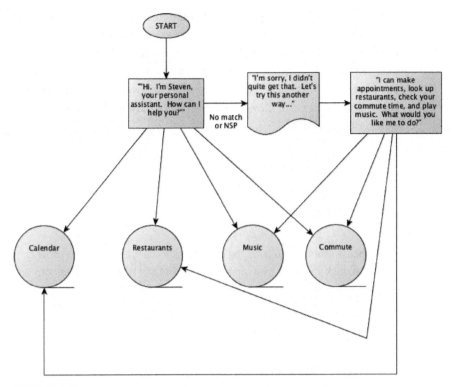

FIGURE 2-6.
Flow for system with more complex branching

In the early IVR days, confirmations were sometimes used to an excessive degree. Here's an example:

IVR TRAVEL SYSTEM
Would you like me to book that flight?

CALLER
Yes, please.

IVR TRAVEL SYSTEM
I think you said "yes." Is that correct?

CALLER
Yes.

IVR TRAVEL SYSTEM
OK, I will book your flight...

A funny example of why over-confirmation can sound so unnatural was highlighted by a *Saturday Night Live* skit from 2006, called "Julie, the Operator Lady." It was a parody between Rachel Dratch (playing the part of Julie, the Amtrak IVR persona) and Antonio Banderas, talking at a party. Ten years later, Amtrak now has an award-winning IVR system—but you can see how the same style of dialog doesn't quite work in the real world:

JULIE
Will you be needing drinks tonight?

ANTONIO BANDERAS
Sure, thanks.

JULIE
Please listen carefully, as the options have changed—or, if you know the drink you want, you can interrupt me at any time. There's merlot, chardonnay, various cocktails—

ANTONIO BANDERAS
Gin and tonic, on the rocks, lime...

JULIE
Before I get your drink, lemme see if I have that right. That's one, gin and tonic, on the rocks, with a twist. Did I get that right?

ANTONIO BANDERAS
Yes.

JULIE
Your approximate wait time is one minute... *[Julie walks away]*

Over-confirming information might ensure accuracy, but it will also drive people (like Antonio Banderas) crazy.

When determining the right confirmation strategy for a VUI experience, consider the following:

- What is the consequence for getting it wrong? (Would the wrong flight end up being booked? Would someone's money be transferred to the wrong account? Would a traveler hear the weather for the wrong city?)

- What modalities will the system have to provide feedback? (Will it be audio-only? Will there be nontextual visual feedback such as the light ring on the Amazon Echo?)

- Will it have a small screen, such as a smartwatch, or a medium-sized screen, such as an iPhone?

- What type of confirmation is most appropriate? (Explicit confirmation? Implicit? A hybrid?)

If someone is transferring money from one place to another, confirmation is extremely important. On the other hand, if the app is purely for entertainment, getting one thing wrong might not be a big deal, and in fact, might break the user out of the experience of the conversation.

Always take advantage of the channels you have available. When you want to talk to the Amazon Echo (by saying "Alexa"), the top rim of the device lights up in blue, letting you know that she's now listening to a command. Note that the Echo is in fact *always* listening, but it does not light up until it knows that you want to initiate a conversation with it. I talk more about how devices show you they're listening in Chapter 5.

When you ask the Amazon Echo a question, its primary channel for output is audio. It does have the aforementioned illuminating ring at the top, but this is generally just to indicate it's listening (or processing), not to give you actual information. In addition, you can access information you give to the Echo on another device—such as your phone—after the fact (e.g., if you asked Alexa to add an item to your shopping list).

For VUI experiences for which audio feedback is the primary method to provide feedback, it is important to craft confirmations carefully. One way to do this is by using *confidence thresholds*.

A confidence threshold is how the speech recognition engine lets you know how well it thinks it's performed. For example, it might recognize that you said "YES, PLEASE"—but the confidence could vary. Perhaps it's only 45 percent confident that this is what it heard, or perhaps it's 85 percent. Your app can access this information, and handle them in different ways:

Explicit confirmation
Force the user to confirm the information. For example, "I think you want to set a reminder to 'buy insurance before going skydiving next week.' Is that right?"

Let the user know what was understood, but do not ask them to confirm. For example, "OK, setting a reminder to buy insurance..." (In the case of implicit confirmation, it might be necessary to allow the user to cancel or go back a step.)

There are many different ways to confirm information. The next section describes them in more detail.

Method 1: Three-Tiered Confidence

In this case, the system will explicitly confirm information between a certain threshold (e.g., 45–80), reject anything with a lower confidence, and implicitly confirm anything above the 80 percent threshold. It's especially important to explicitly confirm information if the cost of a misrecognition (i.e., the system got it wrong) is high. Here is an example of how this might sound:

USER
Please buy more paper towels.

VUI
[>80 percent confidence, implicit confirmation] OK, ordering more paper towels...

[45–79 percent confidence, explicit confirmation] I thought you said you'd like to order more paper towels. Is that correct?

[<45 percent confidence] I'm sorry, I didn't get that. What would you like to buy?

Method 2: Implicit Confirmation

Another method is to only confirm things implicitly, without requiring the user to take action. For example, if I ask, "What's the world's tallest mountain?" a system with implicit confirmation would give me the answer right away: "The world's tallest mountain is Mount Everest." Along with the answer, it included a piece of the original question so that I know the system recognized me.

Some systems provide the answer without confirming the original question; for example, simply saying "Mount Everest." This approach can be appropriate when the confidence is very high and when trying to be more conversational.

Here are some other examples of implicit confirmation:

- "The weather in San Francisco is..."
- "OK, I've set your appointment for 10 AM tomorrow morning."
- "All right, I'll tell you a story..."
- "Cheetahs are the fastest land animal."

Method 3: Nonspeech Confirmation

Another type of confirmation relies on completing an action that does not require a spoken response. For example, imagine that you are creating an app to turn the lights on and off in your home. The user says, "Turn on the Christmas tree lights." Is it really necessary to say, "OK, turning on the Christmas lights," when the lights just turned on?

A couple of caveats to this approach. First, you might want to consider having an audio confirmation that the system heard the user if there is likely to be a delay. For example, if it takes a few seconds for the lights to come on, it is useful to have the system say, "OK," or, "Got it," to let the user know it's going to happen, even though it might take a few seconds. In addition, this lets the user know that if the lights do *not* turn on, it was not that the device did not hear the user. A second use case is if you're doing something for which you won't be able to see it to confirm, such as turning on the oven while you're sitting in another room.

Another type of confirmation that does not use speech but does use audio is an "earcon": a brief, distinctive sound. In the 511 IVR system (which provides traffic and transit information), when the user returns to the main menu, a specific, short audio clip plays. When the user goes to the traffic menu, a short car horn beep is played. This is called *landmarking*, and it helps users to quickly understand they have been taken to the right place.

Method 4: Generic Confirmation

In some conversational systems, it might be appropriate not to confirm exactly what the user said—even implicitly. This applies more for conversational systems in which the user might be doing more open-ended chatting. In this example, an avatar asks how someone is feeling, but does not necessarily act on that information:

> **AVATAR**
> How are you feeling today, Cathy?
>
> **CATHY**
> Well, pretty good today, I guess.
>
> **AVATAR**
> **Thank you for sharing that with me.** How did you sleep last night?
>
> **CATHY**
> Not so great.
>
> **AVATAR**
> I'm sorry to hear that.

This sort of *generic confirmation* can allow for a richer sharing experience from the user. This type of response will allow a wide variety of input from the user, while still moving the conversation along. Keep in mind that in human–human conversations, we don't go around confirming exactly what someone says every time. Sometimes we might say, "mm hmm," or, "tell me more"—and it's OK for a computer to do that, as well.

To keep things more interesting, it helps to randomize these types of generic confirmations.

Note the confirmation in the second piece, as well: when the user says she did not sleep well, the avatar does not say "So you did not sleep well," but rather offers up a sympathetic response. This turn in this conversation could have three categories of responses:

- Slept well ("I slept great," "Good, thanks")
- Slept poorly ("Not so great," "I barely slept," "I slept terribly")
- System is not sure ("Well I dreamed a lot," "I was up late")

There could be a set of appropriate randomized responses for each of these cases.

Method 5: Visual Confirmation

With mobile devices, visual confirmation is a commonly used method. For example, when asking Google a question, it often provides an audio confirmation as well as a visual one (Figure 2-7):

USER
Ok Google. When's my next meeting?

GOOGLE
You have a calendar entry tomorrow. The title is "Chinatown field trip."

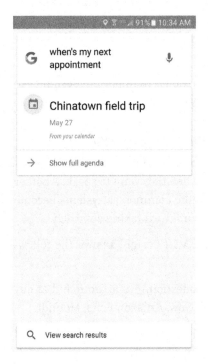

FIGURE 2-7.
Google's visual confirmation of a meeting

Take advantage of the screen! Communicating a list of items is much more effective on a screen. Humans have a limited capacity to remember a string of information; typically, a user can't remember more than about seven auditory items at a time.[2] "The ephemeral nature of output in auditory interfaces places significant cognitive demands on the user."[3]

---

2   Miller, G. "The Magical Number Seven, Plus or Minus Two: Some Limits On Our Capacity for Processing Information," *Psychological Review* (1956).

3   Cohen, M., Giangola, J., and Balogh, J. *Voice User Interface Design*. (Boston, MA: Addison-Wesley, 2004), 75.

However, by putting those same items into a visual list on a screen, the cognitive load is lessened. Now the user can examine the list at their leisure, without remembering each little detail. This also gives the user more time to make a decision.

Another great way to use the screen is for confirming the user's choice. Imagine a system that allows the user to select a response by either speaking or pressing a button. The system asks, "Did you take your antibiotics last night?" and provides a Yes and a No button. The user could say, "Yes," and rather than have the system say, "I think you said 'yes,'" simply highlight the button, as if the user had pressed it. The user will know whether she has been correctly (or incorrectly) understood (Figure 2-8).

In addition to thinking about confirmations, an important design decision is when to allow your user to speak.

Command-and-Control Versus Conversational

Most of the VUI systems out there today are *command and control*, meaning the user must explicitly indicate when they want to speak. Another type of design, which is becoming more common as systems become more conversational, uses a more natural turn-taking approach.

To know which type is right for your VUI design, answer the following questions:

- Can the user ask the system a question/give a command at any time? (For example, Siri, Google Now, Amazon Echo, Hound)

- Will the user be involved in a closed conversation with an explicit beginning and end? (Chatbot, game, avatar)

Command-and-Control

Many systems use this approach whereby users must do something explicit to indicate to the system that they are going to speak. For example, Siri requires the user to press the home button before speaking (or, from the Siri screen, press the microphone soft button (Figure 2-9). Ok Google requires either pressing the microphone icon, or saying "Ok Google" (Figure 2-10). The Amazon Echo has a physical button, but users can also indicate that they are about to speak by saying the wake word, "Alexa." Even the starship *Enterprise* required the crew to say "Computer" before making a request.

FIGURE 2-8.
Users can speak or press buttons to reply to Sensely's avatar

Is this for an urgent issue?

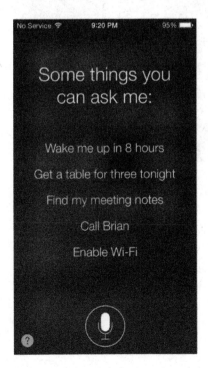

Some things you can ask me:

Wake me up in 8 hours

Get a table for three tonight

Find my meeting notes

Call Brian

Enable Wi-Fi

FIGURE 2-9.
After holding down the home button to activate Siri and then failing, the microphone button appears

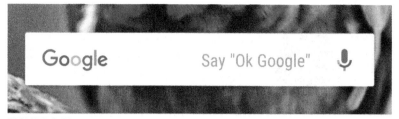

FIGURE 2-10.
To speak to Google, say "Ok Google" or tap microphone button

In many cars, the user must use a "push-to-talk" approach; that is, the driver must press a specific physical button on the steering wheel to indicate that they will speak (Figure 2-11).

FIGURE 2-11.
The push-to-talk button in the Toyota Matrix (photo by author)

When this happens, the system typically responds with either nonverbal audio (the "bonk" noise) and/or with visual feedback (a wavy line, animated dots, a glowing light on the device). The user then knows that the system is listening and can speak (Figure 2-12).

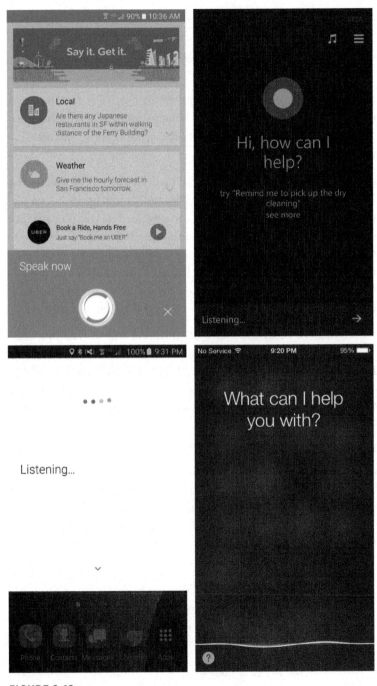

FIGURE 2-12.

Listening indicators: (from upper left to bottom) Hound, Cortana, Google, and Siri

When the system has decided that the user has finished speaking, it indicates in some way, often with more nonverbal audio (the "up" noise from Siri), and then responds. Identifying when the user has stopped speaking is called *endpoint detection*; I discuss this in more detail in Chapter 4.

At this point, the conversation might well be over. The system is not expecting the user to speak again, although sometimes it can handle a related follow-up request. *But the user must again explicitly indicate that they are going to speak.*

This works well for situations in which the device has no idea when the user might speak. Imagine you're in the family room and your spouse is in the kitchen. You haven't spoken for a while. You will probably use some kind of explicit notification to your spouse to let them know you're going to speak, such as, "Hey, honey, can I ask you a question?" or, "Hey, Chris." This prepares your spouse to listen. If you went for 30 minutes without speaking and suddenly you said "Where is it?" without any context of what you were looking for, your spouse will likely be confused.

The time window in which your system should still be listening after the wake word or button push should be carefully chosen. Too short, and you'll miss users who hesitate briefly before speaking; too long and the system might be listening to a conversation that's not intended for it. As a rule of thumb, 10 seconds is a good starting point.

Conversational

When there will be a longer back-and-forth between the user and the VUI, forcing the user to explicitly indicate that they are going to talk is not necessary and can be cumbersome and unnatural. When you are in the middle of a conversation with a real person, you do not have to give these indicators at every turn, as demonstrated here:

YOU
Long time no see! How are you doing?

FRIEND
I am going to speak now. I'm good, how are you?

YOU
Fine. Where did you go last night?

FRIEND
I will now tell you where I went last night. I went to a meetup about bonobos.

That's going to be an awkward conversation.

If your user is involved in a conversation with your app, don't force them to keep indicating they are going to talk. Instead, use natural turn-taking techniques, such as the following:

- Asking a question
- Using eye contact (if you have an avatar or video)
- Pauses
- Explicit direction

The easiest and most natural technique is asking a question. When the VUI asks the user something, people will naturally respond.

Explicit direction is fine, as well. For example, "Why don't you just *tell* me the name of the movie you want to see."

Be careful not to force the user into this conversational mode when it's not appropriate. One virtual assistant I tried would turn the mic back on every time it finished speaking, but it was very confusing.

VIRTUAL ASSISTANT
I'd be happy to look up that info for you. All you have to do is ask.
[turns on mic and beeps]

ME
[thinking...Isn't that what I just did?]

Human turn-taking is not always clear cut. In many cases, a turn might be someone simply making an "mm hmm" noise while the other person continues to talk. As Urban says, a lot of human–human conversations have overlapping turns; when I murmur "mm hmm," it's not a signal that I want the other person to stop talking and give me the conch. Instead, it's a "liveness" indicator—I'm still here, I'm still listening.

Computers are not yet able to handle this more-subtle form of turn-taking. In systems that don't allow users to interrupt, however, this can be workable, since the "mm hmm" will not trigger the recognizer while the system is still talking.

With more careful design, a VUI system can handle some of the more common forms of these subtleties; for example, users might say, "thank you," at the end of a transaction. You can program the system to either ignore this or acknowledge it with a "you're welcome" rather than generate an error/reprompt.

In addition, don't ask rhetorical questions to which you can't understand the answer. Ben Brown, cofounder of "Howdy," a chatbot that runs within the office communication tool Slack, had to outlaw the bot from asking rhetorical questions "because people expect to respond to them, even though the bot was just being polite," he says. "You would never just stick a form on your web page and not expect people to type into it."[4]

Another way you can violate turn-taking is by asking the question before the system has finished speaking. For example, a common IVR structure is, "Would you like to hear that again? You can say 'yes,' 'no,' or 'repeat.'" Users often begin to speak as soon as the question has finished, which leads to frustration because either they can't interrupt, or they interrupt just as the system begins the next sentence, stop talking, and have interrupted the flow. With good prompt design and very careful voice coaching it is possible to make this work, but in general you should avoid it by putting the instruction first and the question at the end.

Sometimes, it makes sense to switch between command-and-control and conversational modes, though it's important to do this only in situations in which users will implicitly understand that the mode has changed. A good example of this is the *Jeopardy!* game on the Amazon Echo. To initiate the game, you must say, "Alexa, start *Jeopardy!*." After Alexa says the quiz answer, however, you do not need to say "Alexa" again—you can simply say the question (e.g., "Who is Dorothy Hamill?") and Alexa will tell you if you're wrong or right. There is no "beep" to let you know you can speak, but there is no need for one—it's a known conversational structure, so users do not have trouble figuring it out.

---

4 Pavlus, J. (2016). "The Next Phase Of UX: Designing Chatbot Personalities." Retrieved from *https://www.fastcodesign.com/*.

Conversational Markers

Another way to make your VUI more human-like (as well as more engaging) is to use conversational markers. See if you can spot the difference between these conversations:

VIRTUAL ASSISTANT
How many hours of sleep did you get last night?

USER
About seven.

VIRTUAL ASSISTANT
How many servings of fruits and vegetables did you eat yesterday?

USER
Maybe four.

VIRTUAL ASSISTANT
Did you take your medication last night?

USER
Yes.

VIRTUAL ASSISTANT
Goodbye.

Versus:

VIRTUAL ASSISTANT
I'll be asking you a few questions about your health. First, how many hours of sleep did you get last night?

USER
About seven.

VIRTUAL ASSISTANT.
Good job. And how many servings of fruits and vegetables did you eat yesterday?

USER
Maybe four.

VIRTUAL ASSISTANT

Got it. Last question—were you able to take your medication last night?

USER

Yes.

VIRTUAL ASSISTANT

All right. That's it for now. I'll talk to you again tomorrow. Goodbye.

Both of these examples collected the same three pieces of information. But which virtual assistant do you think the user will prefer speaking with, day after day?

Conversational markers are an important way to let the user know where they're at in the conversation, and that they are understood. Users will also be more engaged when the system is using basic manners and will respond in kind. They are often the "glue" that keeps the various required pieces of the interaction together.

Conversational markers include:

- Timelines ("First," "Halfway there," and "Finally")

- Acknowledgments ("Thanks," "Got it," "Alright," and "Sorry about that.")

- Positive feedback ("Good job," and "Nice to hear that")

One practical way to see where conversational markers should be added to your dialog is to do a "table read" with someone. Write down a sample dialog (the back and forth between the system and the user) and each of you read one part. You'll quickly see where things might be stilted or unnatural, or add to a user's frustration because they have no idea how long the conversation is going to last.

Here are a couple of common concerns I hear from clients: "Computers don't speak that way," and "People will be put off because it's a computer, not a person." Some clients worry that the system will sound too informal or annoy people by pretending to be human.

It is important to use conversational markers that are appropriate to your system's persona, but even the most formal systems will benefit. Users know they're speaking to a machine, but humans appreciate these conversational basics nonetheless.

Next, we'll discuss a crucial piece of design that addresses something that you hope never happens but is essential nonetheless.

Error Handling

When you talk to a human being, there is never an unrecoverable error state.

ABI JONES, DESIGN LEAD AT GOOGLE

In the traditional IVR world, if the user was not heard or understood, the system prompts the user to speak again. This is important because otherwise the user might think the phone call was cut off or the system isn't functioning. Another reason is that there is a fixed dialog that is expected; at any given point, the user is required to provide input to move the conversation forward. If the system doesn't hear anything, it times out and prompts the user to speak again. If these timeouts are not planned carefully, the user and the system often end up cutting each other off, resulting in an awkward back and forth.

In the mobile VUI and device world, however, it's not always necessary to reprompt the user when there is a failure. The Amazon Echo, for example, does nothing if it doesn't hear you after saying the wake word. (If it heard but did not understand, it plays a short sound.)

When speaking to a device (especially a device with a name), users are more likely to respond to silence the same way they would with a human—by repeating themselves. In addition, the system is not waiting for the next piece of the conversation, because this is often a one-off command. Therefore, if the system fails to respond, it's not that the entire transaction fails—just that one particular command. It's not the same as suddenly ending a conversation in the middle of an important transaction; it has just failed once. Because of the higher fault tolerance, it's more forgiving for Alexa to ignore you when she did not understand.

Imagine, however, that your app said, "I'm sorry, I didn't understand," every time it failed to recognize your latest command. It would get old very quickly. "I didn't understand, I didn't understand, I didn't understand." Alright, already! Users can quickly grow accustomed to a mode in which they simply need to repeat themselves if the device doesn't understand on the first try.

We've talked a lot about "best path" behavior for a VUI design. But, as any good designer knows, you can't just design for when things work—you need to design for when things go wrong, as well. This is especially true with VUIs, because something will always go wrong.

Although speech recognition has improved drastically in the past 10 years (greater than 90 percent accuracy given the right conditions), this will in no way ensure that your users will have a good experience when you add voice to your design. Think for a moment about human-to-human conversation. We often miss a word (or multiple words) when someone else is talking.

All of these factors play a role in VUI, as well. But humans are much better than computers about getting back on track, thanks to a rich understanding of context, and being able to recover from conversational errors. If I say something to you, and you stare at me quizzically, I'm likely to repeat myself, knowing you did not understand. I can ask you to repeat yourself. I can ask you to clarify. We have many ways to course-correct, because we're both steeped in years of practice of human conversation.

When the VUI does not understand us, things often break down. How you decide to handle these error conditions in your VUI is extremely important. As Pilar Manchon, GM of voice and digital assistants at Intel said, "Every time that you score down because you make a mistake, or you don't know something, it actually counts a hundred times for every time that you had it right."[5]

If you do a good job, error conditions won't derail users, and you can get them back on track and have them successfully complete a task. Handle it poorly, and not only will they fail to complete their tasks, they're not likely to come back.

There are a variety of ways VUIs can make mistakes:

- No speech detected
- Speech detected, but nothing recognized
- Something was recognized correctly, but the system does the wrong thing with it
- Something was recognized incorrectly

---

5   Manchon, P. (2016). Quote from her talk at the RE-WORK Virtual Assistant Summit in San Francisco.

No Speech Detected

Speech recognition engines have a "listening" mode in which they attempt to capture a speech signal. If speech is expected but not detected, automated speech recognizers return a "no speech" response.

It's important to keep in mind that this does not necessarily mean that the user didn't say anything. It could be that the user spoke, but for whatever reason, the system did not pick it up.

There are two ways to handle the case of "no speech":

- Call it out explicitly (e.g., "I'm sorry, I didn't hear anything. What is your account number?").

- Do nothing.

Which one should you use? It depends on your app. For the explicit case, the following should be true:

- Your system is audio only (such as an IVR).

- There is no other way for users to respond (such as touching buttons on their mobile phone).

- The system needs a response from the user before it can continue the task/conversation.

There are also cases for which it's appropriate to do nothing:

- The user can move forward another way (such as choosing a response via a button).

- The consequence of not acting does not break the conversation.

- There is a visual indicator that the system did not understand, such as an avatar continuing to engage in active listening by looking at the user.

Why not just err on the side of caution and always prompt the user to speak again? Because it becomes very annoying. Humans have a variety of ways to indicate that they did not understand what was said, and one of the most common (and effective) is to say nothing. Instead, you might look quizzically at the person, or smile politely—this action makes it clear very quickly that the speaker was either not heard or not understood.

VUI designers should take advantage of conversational rules that humans are already comfortable with. Rather than continually telling the user they were not understood (and having them lose faith in the system), subtle cues can be just as effective.

When conducting user tests at Volio, I have observed cases in which this was so well done that users did not even remember afterward an error had occurred, even when asked. In this case, when the user was not understood, the video showed the actor simply continuing to listen—nothing else occurred. The users naturally repeated themselves, and the system moved on.

Speech Detected but Nothing Recognized

In some cases, the automated speech recognition (ASR) tool did detect an audio signal, but it was unable to come up with any reliable hypotheses.

The strategies for dealing with this case are very similar to the case of "no speech detected":

- Call it out explicitly (e.g., "I'm sorry, I didn't get that. What was the name of the restaurant?" or "Sorry, what was that?").

- Do nothing.

Some systems attempt to be clever or funny. If Alexa knows you were asking a question, but doesn't have a way to answer it, she replies, "I'm sorry, I didn't understand the question I heard."

Siri, in some instances in which the system does not understand—for example, "Siri, tell me the meaning of love,"—will reply, "Who, me?"

Be careful with these types of responses. "Who, me?" can be cute the first couple of times, but I've seen users become exasperated with this nonhelpful response.

Recognized but Not Handled

In this case, the ASR tool did return a perfectly accurate recognition result, but for whatever reason, your VUI did not handle it properly. This could be because you did not program in a response. It could also be that you programmed the wrong response. Here's an example:

MEDICAL VIRTUAL ASSISTANT
How are you feeling?

USER
I have a cold.

MEDICAL VIRTUAL ASSISTANT
How long have you been feeling cold?

In this example, the system decided that the keyword "cold" meant temperature, and now the conversation has been derailed. A smarter system would look for the concept of "having a cold" versus "being cold."

Another example is when the system recognized it perfectly but has no programmed response:

MEDICAL VIRTUAL ASSISTANT
How are you feeling?

USER
Uh, my arm sort of hurts.

MEDICAL VIRTUAL ASSISTANT
I'm sorry, I didn't get that. How did you say you're feeling?

This is a case in which whoever designed the types of responses the system could handle did not include one for arm pain.

The strategy for handling these? Better anticipation of all the things a user might say. For tips on how to avoid this issue through data collection, see Chapter 5.

Recognized but Incorrectly

This is the case in which the ASR tool returned the wrong recognition result. This could produce two outcomes: either you don't do anything with it, because you don't expect it, or it incorrectly matches to the wrong behavior. Let's look at an example:

MEETING SCHEDULING VA
What time would you like to schedule your meeting with Sharon?

USER
Umm...well, I guess I'd like to sort of, umm...I will schedule it for 3:30.

MEETING SCHEDULING VA
[ASR tool returned "um well I guess I'd like to sort of um I will sledge it throw forty"]
I'm sorry, what time did you say?

Unfortunately, there is not a lot you can do about the ASR tool not recognizing things correctly; however, you can build in ways to work around this issue by using *N*-best lists and data analysis of real user responses. (An *N*-best list is the list of the top possible recognition results returned by the ASR tool—for more about *N*-best lists, see Chapter 4.)

Escalating Error

A common strategy for cases when speech is expected (and is the primary mode for communicating with the app) is to use escalating error strategies. This simple example reminds the user what the needed information is:

WEATHER APP
I can get the weather for you. What's the city and state?

USER
Uhhh...it's Springfield.

WEATHER APP
I'm sorry, I didn't get that. Please say the city and state.

USER
Oh, it's Springfield, Minnesota.

Escalating error behavior prompts can become more detailed if needed, offering more help such as where to find an account number. In addition, if after several turns speech has continued to fail, offer another mode of communication such as pressing buttons or using a drop-down list of options.

Here's an example showing a flight lookup app in which the user enters a number but it's the reservation confirmation number, not the flight number. Rather than just reasking for the flight number, the system reminds the user what the number looks like:

AIRLINE APP
Please tell me your flight number, and I'll look up the reservation.

USER
Uhh...576782.

AIRLINE APP

I'm sorry, I don't recognize that. Your flight number is three digits long and follows the letters UA.

USER

Oh, that! It's 375.

AIRLINE APP

Thank you. Getting your reservation...

If you are working on a system in which there is a live person who can provide assistance, set a threshold for number of errors, and when that threshold is met, transfer the user to the live assistance.

Don't Blame the User

When at all possible, do not blame the user. Blame it on something else, or at the very least blame the system.

In a study performed by Clifford Nass and Scott Brave, users performed tasks with a driving simulator, and throughout the tasks, the system voice made comments about their driving performance. Half of the participants heard messages blaming the driver ("You're driving too fast.") and half heard messages blaming external factors, such as "Steering is difficult on this road."[6]

The participants who were blamed by the system rated their driving performance lower, liked the voice less, and most importantly, showed less attention while driving. Error messages might seem like a small thing, but they can affect the user's perception of the system and even their performance.

Novice and Expert Users

If your users will be using your system on a regular basis, it's important to include different strategies in the design.

For example, a healthcare app might require users to log in every day and take their blood pressure. In the beginning, having the prompts include more instructional details is useful and necessary. However,

---

6   Nass, C., and Brave, S. *Wired for Speech.* (Cambridge, MA: The MIT Press, 2005), 125

after the user has become familiar with the app, there is no need to continue lengthy instructions (as well as other prompts). Let's take a look at an example of each scenario.

Novice user:

> **AVATAR**
> Let's take your blood pressure. Please make sure the cuff is turned on. Wrap the cuff around your arm so that the blue arrow is pointing toward your palm. Be sure to sit down and have your feet flat on the floor. When you're ready, press continue.

User has interacted with the app every day for a week:

> **AVATAR**
> Time to take your blood pressure. Please put the cuff on and press continue.

Don't just count the number of times the app has been used, however. It might be that an individual has used it many times but only once every month or two. In this case, you would continue to use the novice prompts.

You can also shorten explanatory prompts. For example, the system might say, "I'll be asking you a series of questions about how you're feeling. It will take a few minutes, but the questions will help the doctor determine the best course of action. First, did you take your medication yesterday?"

After doing this every other day for a week, you can shorten it to, "Did you take your medication yesterday?" (Be sure to use "conversational markers" even though the prompts are shorter, to keep the user informed that their answers have been understood, and where they are in the set of questions.)

Margaret Urban, interaction designer at Google, says it's important to ensure that your goal is not simply to "train" your user. She says rather than beat them over the head with the available commands, adapt to *their* behavior.

In addition, take advantage of the concept of *priming*. Priming refers to the fact that exposing someone to a particular stimulus (such as a word or image) will influence their response to a later stimulus. For example, if you've been watching a nature program about llamas in Peru, and afterward someone asks you to name an animal that begins with the letter "L," you're much more likely to say llama than lion.

Letting someone know up front that you'll be asking them a certain number of questions is also a form of priming; it gives the person an indication of what to expect, so they know how to prepare themselves.

Priming can be subtler. If your VUI confirms commands in a certain way, it primes the user to phrase it similarly in the future. For example, if I say, "I would like to hear the song by the group the Barenaked Ladies that's called 'Call and Answer,'" and my VUI responds with, "Playing 'Call and Answer' by the Barenaked Ladies," next time I might just say, "play 'Call and Answer' by the Barenaked Ladies," instead.

Keeping Track of Context

Remember the earlier example in which Google was able to continue the conversation about Abraham Lincoln? Let's take a look at it again:

USER
Ok Google. Who was the 16th president of the United States?

GOOGLE
Abraham Lincoln was the 16th president of the United States.

USER
How old was he when he died?

GOOGLE
Abraham Lincoln died at the age of 56.

USER
Where was he born?

GOOGLE
Hodgenville, KY.

USER
What is the best restaurant there?

GOOGLE
Here is Paula's Hot Biscuit.

What's good about this example? Google continued the conversation, and remembered the context. Specifically, the use of pronouns. It knew "he" referred to Abraham Lincoln. It also knew that "there" meant Hodgenville, Kentucky. Keeping track of this information is not always easy, but without it, your app won't be capable of anything but one-turn actions. The use of two different terms to refer to the same thing is called *coreference*, and is an essential part of communication. Without it, conversations will quickly break down.

Here's another example, though a fictitious one, about an app that can help find movies to watch on TV:

USER
Show me movies with Harrison Ford.

TV
[shows list of movies starring Harrison Ford]

USER
Which ones were made before 1990?

TV
[shows new list]

USER
Now show me movies with him and Carrie Fisher.

TV
[shows list]

In this case, the app needs to know what "ones" means as well as "him."

It can be difficult to anticipate all the things your system might need to track, but you can begin with the basics and build up based on what your users are actually saying (see more in Chapter 5).

If the user asks a question about a person, store that information. If the person is famous, you can even look up the gender. However, you can also use a simpler method, which is to always store the last person mentioned, and refer to that person whether the user says 'he' or 'she.' (Of course, this will not work if the user has mentioned more than one person, but in many instances it will work just fine.)" If you can't determine the gender, you can also just use the person's name, although it can sound robotic to keep using the full name rather than a pronoun. "They," the gender-neutral form, is also gaining acceptance.

You can apply similar processes to remembering the last city or place the user (or the system) mentioned.

Systems often struggle with interpreting the user's references. Here's a Cortana example that isn't able to handle the second query in the conversation:

USER
What's the most expensive dog?

CORTANA

USER
Where can I get one?

CORTANA

As you can see, Cortana did not assign a meaning to "one" and treated the query as brand new. To contrast this, look at what Google does:

USER

What's the most expensive dog?

GOOGLE

According to PopSugar, the most expensive dog in the global world today is the Tibetan Mastiff.

USER

Where can I get one?

GOOGLE

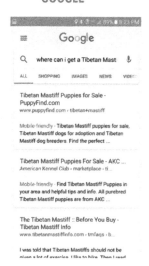

Here, Google successfully understood the word "one" in the second query, and gave some relevant search results.

Help and Other Universals

When I worked on IVR systems, we made sure to include a set of universals at every state: repeat, main menu, help, operator, and goodbye.

For mobile apps, this is not a hard-and-fast rule. Many mobile apps (or connected devices) do not have the concept of a main menu. However, it is still important to ensure that users can get help when needed.

Supporting the "help" command is useful in many cases, but is traditionally used for context-specific help. For example, imagine an insurance IVR system in which a user has been asked to enter their medical record number (MRN). If the user says, "help," at this point, it would be useful to remind the user that the MRN is on their insurance card.

But what if the user asks for help in an open-ended situation such as a general assistant, like Google, Cortana, or Siri? If the user has just initiated the conversation (by pressing the home button or saying, "Ok Google," and then says "help"), you have no context around which to know what type of help the user needs.

In addition, users are not always accustomed to using these types of universal phrases, despite us IVR designers trying to train them for many years! Therefore, it's important to think not only about what type of help to provide, but how users might say it. For example, "Alexa, what can you do?" or asking Cortana, "What can you do for me?" Or with Google, asking, "Ok Google, what can I say to you?" In fact, Ok Google will display examples if you simply tap the mic and say nothing.

Alexa doesn't even try to handle that question on her own; instead, she says, "For help with what you can say, take a look at the 'things to try section' in the Alexa app."

Cortana says "Here are some things I can help you do" and provides a visual set of examples, depicted in Figure 2-13.

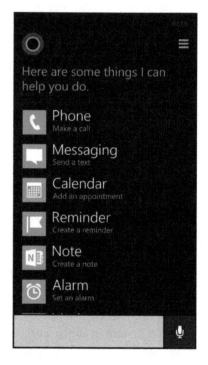

FIGURE 2-13.
Cortana lists visual examples of possible voice commands

Google says nothing, but provides a screen of examples, as shown in Figure 2-14.

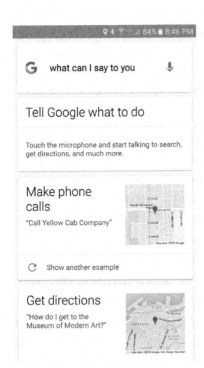

In addition to allowing users to ask for help, take advantage of visual space if you have it, such as on a mobile app. Imagine designing an adventure game in which the player can talk to various characters and explore different worlds. Having a "help" or "info" button always available in the GUI commands is an obvious way to let the user know assistance is available.

In the current world of VUIs, "help" (and other ways people can ask "What can I do here?") is especially important because there is no all-powerful VUI out there. Despite many VUIs saying something very open, such as "How may I help you?" they are still very limited in what they can understand and act on. Users need a way to find out just what it is they can really do.

Another important piece of good IVR design was to include a "good-bye" universal. In the early VUI designs, goodbye was not considered important because people could simply hang up to end the conversation. But years of collecting data made designers realize that, because people were used to saying goodbye to people when ending a phone conversation, they often did it with IVR systems, as well, and sometimes felt uncomfortable ending conversations by simply hanging up. Therefore, we added dialog to handle this case. Another important lesson was to make sure the system was *very* confident before actually hanging up! If your system will be using a "goodbye" option, be sure to use three-tiered confidence and confirm that the user really wants to exit the system if confidence is not high.

Here's an example from the 511 IVR system, when confidence was medium: "I thought I heard you say goodbye. Do you really want to exit the system?"

The other night on my way to bed, I passed by my Amazon Echo and said, "Alexa, good night." She responded with "Good night." It might sound like a silly thing in which to invest development time, but it was very satisfying.

Allowing users to repeat and to go back a step are important for conversational systems as well. "Go back" is not necessary for things like Google Now, in which interactions are short, but for a task-oriented conversation, go back is very useful. During tasks that are not within a set of conversational turns, "go back" can take on different meanings. For example, if your user is listening to music, it might indicate they want to hear a previous song. These are commands that are often good candidates for GUI controls, as well.

Latency

Another component that is sometimes missed by designers is latency. It is important to determine as early as possible whether or not your system will have any latency, or delays. Latencies are generally caused by:

- Poor connectivity
- System processing
- Database access

Perhaps your VUI system needs to access patient records, and you know that this will require a database lookup. Find out as early as possible how long this is likely to be, and plan accordingly.

If there is a known latency, ensure that the system has a way to handle this. You can do this both by the system telling the user about the delay ("One moment while I look up your record...") as well as nonverbal and visual cues, such as a latency noise (often used on IVR systems) and visual (animated loading icon), as demonstrated in Figure 2-15.

FIGURE 2-15.

Sensely avatar says "One moment please," displays the message, and shows the loading GIF

One moment please...

There might be cases in which the expected latency time could range from none to 10 seconds. If so, in the case of no latency, pad the latency by a few seconds, because it sounds broken to the user if you say "One moment please" and immediately continue the conversation. If you set up the expectation of a delay, do not violate that expectation.

Sometimes latency can occur when processing speech, as well. Many devices use local recognition for their wake word, which is fast, and then send the rest of the audio for processing on the cloud.

Disambiguation

There can be times when the user provides some but not all of the details to take an action. For example, the user might ask for the weather for a location that exists in more than one place: "What's the weather in Springfield?"

If possible, rely on any known information to determine the answer without having to ask the user. For example, the Amazon Echo requires the user to specify the home location as a part of the set up; thus, when you ask, "What's the weather?" Alexa produces local conditions automatically. Knowing the home location can be used when the user asks for the weather somewhere else, as well—for instance, choose the "Springfield" close to home rather than across the country.

Other contextual clues can also be used. If the user just looked up a restaurant in Springfield, Illinois, and then asks, "What's the weather in Springfield?" you can pretty safely bet that they mean the one in the location they just referenced.

If no contextual information is available, the system will need to ask the user to clarify:

> USER
> What's the weather in Springfield?
>
> SYSTEM
> Did you mean the one in Illinois, or Maryland?
>
> USER
> Illinois.
>
> SYSTEM
> It's 65 degrees...

If the system has high confidence for the word "Springfield," it can use the reference word "one" rather than explicitly stating the name again. Also, be sure to allow the user flexibility in their response: the user should be able to say "Springfield, Illinois" or just "Illinois" or even "the first one" (imagine a list).

Another example where disambiguation is required is when an action is not clear:

> **USER**
> Call Cindy, please.
>
> **SYSTEM**
> OK. Cell phone, or home phone?
>
> **USER**
> Cell phone.
>
> **SYSTEM**
> Calling Cindy, cell phone...

Note the confirmation of the name came at the end, as an implicit conversation. This would be done if the system had (a) high confidence about the name and (b) there was only one Cindy in the caller's Contacts list.

I noticed Google recently improved its dialing design. It used to be that when I said, "Text Chris Leggetter," Google responded with, "Home or mobile?" and I had to choose. Now it's smart enough to know I meant mobile, because I can't text a home phone number.

Disambiguation might also be required when the user answers with more information than your VUI can handle.

> **SYSTEM**
> What is your main symptom?
>
> **USER**
> I'm throwing up and I have a fever.
>
> **SYSTEM**
> OK. Which one would you say is your *primary* symptom?
>
> **USER**
> Uh, my fever I guess.
>
> **SYSTEM**
> OK, fever...

It would be ideal if your system could handle both symptoms at the same time, but given that these systems do have underlying constraints, sometimes it is necessary to ask the user to narrow it down.

Design Documentation

In addition to the previously mentioned sample dialogs and dialog flow document, there are other tangible things that you might need to think about.

Prompts

It might be necessary during the design to create lists of prompts. A "prompt" is what the system can say to the user. It can be a complete sentence or sentences ("I can help you with that. Please tell me the make and model of your car.") or it might be smaller snippets, such as numbers, dates, or products.

Prompt lists serve multiple purposes:

- A list for voice talent to record

- Getting sign off from the client

- Input to the TTS engine

For a great resource on what prompt lists should look like, and how to create prompt lists for concatenation, see the previously referenced book, *Voice User Interface Design*.

Grammars/Key Phrases

In the early IVR days, we needed to specify complete grammars for every state in the dialog. For example, if the prompt asked the user "Do you want me to book the flight?" the grammar might look like this:

Yes: { "yep," "yeah," "uh huh," "sure," "yes yes," "yes book the flight"}, and so on.

In addition, it needs filler words, such as "um" and "uh" and pleasantries such as "please" and "thanks."

Because of the improvements of speech recognition technology, this is thankfully no longer the case. Instead, a lot of systems can get by with specifying key phrases instead of exact sentences, or using machine learning (starting with a set of sample input) to map the user's intent.

I'll get into more details on how to interpret natural language in Chapter 5.

Accessibility

To discuss accessibility, I've brought in an expert: Chris Maury. Maury is the founder of Conversant Labs, a company focused on improving the lives of the blind through providing improved access to technology. In 2011, Maury was told that he was going blind. Maury turned to technology to begin preparing for this future, but was dismayed at what was (or was not) available. Maury quickly realized that standard accessibility technology such as screen readers were not always pleasant to use. As Maury wrote:

> From the beginning, I hated the way that Screen Readers work. Why are they designed the way they are? It makes no sense to present information visually and then, and only then, translate that into audio. All of the time and energy that goes into creating the perfect user experience for an app is wasted, or even worse, adversely impacting the experience for blind users.[7]

He set out to design audio experiences from scratch. In the sections that follow, he offers some tips on how to do just that.

Although designing experiences for everyone, no matter their abilities, should be a core requirement in every project, it becomes especially meaningful as we begin to explore interactions that go beyond a touchscreen and keyboard. What is a VUI but the ideal, nonvisual experience for the blind and visually impaired? The constraints of designing for people with different disabilities can help to inform how we solve

---

7   Maury, C. (2016). "War Stories: My Journey From Blindness to Building a Fully Conversational User Interface." Retrieved from *https://backchannel.com/*.

similar challenges in not just VUI design but other emerging arenas, as well: conversational applications (chatbots) and immersive computing (virtual and augmented reality).

Here are a few best practices for VUI design informed by accessibility:

- Interactions should be time efficient.

- They should provide context.

- They should prioritize personalization over personality.

Interaction Should Be Time-Efficient

When designing visual experiences, we try to limit the number of clicks a user must take to complete an action. The more clicks, the more cumbersome and tedious the experience feels. The same holds for voice-driven interaction, as well. Imagine asking a user for their address:

APP
What is your street address?

USER
1600 Pennsylvania Avenue

APP
What city?

USER
Washington

APP
What state?

USER
DC

APP
And what is your zip code?

USER
20009

In this example, the user must go through four call and responses before completing a single task. Now compare that to a single interaction:

APP
What is your complete address?

Pennsylvania Ave, Washington, DC 20009.

This time there is only a single interaction. Although you might want to have a confirmation prompt ("I heard you say 1600 Pennsylvania Ave. Is that correct?"), there are still half as many interactions to complete the same task, making the design feel more responsive.

Keep It Short

In a visual experience, users can quickly focus their attention to the information that is most relevant to them, skipping over sections of the interface that they don't care about. Audio interfaces, on the other hand, are linear. There is no skipping around. You are forced to listen to everything the app decides to tell you. This being the case, keep it short. Limit text to the most important information, and within that, present the most important information first.

In the example of a shopping app, imagine the user is listening to search results for a given product. Present the title of the product, the price, and the rating. Everything else can be deferred to a single product details dialog, as illustrated in Figure 2-16:

"Harry Potter and the Cursed Child by J.K. Rowling" — $17.99 — 3.5 out of 5 stars

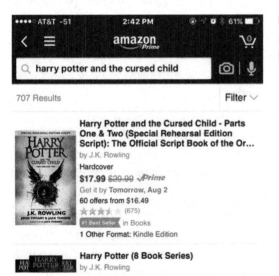

FIGURE 2-16.
Amazon book sample page for Harry Potter

Compare this to the visual experience, which can cram in far more details into a single search result, even on mobile.

For information that doesn't make the cut, allow the user to ask for it. Continuing with the shopping example, here are some possible other queries the user might have:

- "What are the product specifications?"
- "Read me the reviews"
- "Is it hardcover or paperback?"

Talk Faster!

A well-designed interface should have a shallow learning curve while still providing advanced features for power users (drop-down menus versus keyboard shortcuts). These advanced features make the interface significantly more time-efficient for those users who have the skills to use them. Many blind users of screen readers have trained themselves to listen to text at exceedingly fast speeds. You can listen to a demonstration at *https://www.youtube.com/watch?v=92pM6hJG6Wo*.

Not only can you read a book in less than half the time, but you can navigate voice-based applications significantly faster, as well. Not every user is going to be able to listen to your app at 950 words per minute, but more and more users are becoming accustomed to higher than normal speeds. For example, users can increase the playback speed on any YouTube videos up to 2 times, and the video speed controller extension for Chrome, which can increase playback speeds up to 5 times has more than 125,000 downloads.

Let your users control the speech rate of your app. It is a power feature that not every user will take advantage of, but it will make your app feel significantly more responsive to those users who can. Imagine what the world would be like if Photoshop didn't support keyboard shortcuts.

Interrupt Me at Any Time

In graphical applications, when the app is loading, the user is waiting. They can't do anything until everything is ready. The equivalent wait time in VUIs is waiting for the application to respond—recognizing what the user said and understanding what they meant are time-intensive processes. Don't add to this wait time by forcing the user to wait for the app to finish speaking. (Allowing users to interrupt the system in this way is called *barge-in*.)

If you have an app that allows users to search nearby businesses, don't make them listen to all search results before selecting the one that they heard:

> **USER**
> What coffee shops are nearby?
>
> **APP**
> There are four coffee shops within a 10-minute walk.
>
> Espresso a Mano, 4 out of 5 stars, 2-minute walk.
>
> Starbucks, 3.5 out of 5 stars.
>
> **USER**
> Give me directions to Espresso a Mano.

Another good example is asking Alexa for the weather. She begins with the most relevant information and then goes on to provide more detail. The user can say, "Alexa, stop," at any time.

Provide Context

One of the primary challenges in VUI design is educating users on what they can do. In graphical applications, this is less of a problem. Everything is right there on the screen. You can see which buttons you can tap and which menus you can click. For voice interfaces, this visual discovery of features is nonexistent. The design of the VUI should inform the user as to how they can respond or what actions they can take.

When prompting the user, the text of the prompt should help to inform the user how they should respond, or specific actions they can take:

- "Here are four recipes for ratatouille. You can ask me for more information on any of them."

- "You are standing in an open field west of a white house, with a boarded front door; there is a mail box here."

But this implied context is often not enough, or a user might forget what they were doing. In these instances, they should be able to fall back to an explicit orientation action.

Where Am I?

A user should be able to ask for help at any time, and the help message should reorient them to their current context within the application. Here are some common user expressions of confusion:

- "Help"
- "What can I say?"
- "Where am I?"
- "Umm, I'm confused"
- [silence] (after an app prompts the user for input).

And here are some example help messages:

- "You can say 'search' at any time to search for a new product."
- "Your next meeting is at noon. Did you want me to remind you 10 minutes before?"

Help messages should reorient the user to the current context of the conversation as well as prompt them for common next steps.

Text-to-Speech Personalization

Allow users to choose what text-to-speech voice (TTS) voice that they will listen to in the app. Not only do these voices have their own unique personalities that can align with the brand of your specific application (think of a cooking app with the voice of Gordon Ramsey), but they can have technical features that users might prefer. Many voices are built with high speech rates in mind; they can sound more robotic, but they are much more intelligible at higher words per minute. In addition, users might have preferences for different voices, and simply enjoy using some more than others.

Other Types of Accessibility

Sara Basson, accessibility evangelist, and Nandini Stocker, voice user interface designer, both at Google, also contributed their thoughts on VUIs for accessibility:

When we think of "disabilities," we often think of "visible" disabilities that are easy to identify, such as motor impairments, visual impairments, and deafness. There are additional disabilities that might be less apparent, such as cognitive disabilities. These include ADHD, dyslexia, and the autism spectrum, as well as other intellectual disabilities. Even "visible" disabilities cover a broad swath, and include varying degrees of hearing loss, and motor impairments like carpal tunnel syndrome and muscle weakness. Statistics suggest that 15 to 20 percent of the world's population has some disability. Clearly this is a population to consider seriously when designing voice user interfaces, given the prevalence of disabilities and also because it's the right thing to do.

Creating systems with voice input and output can be an enabling option for users who are visually or motor impaired. Users with visual impairments might find services easier to use with voice commands, particularly if the alternative interface is a touchscreen that does not provide verbal feedback. Speech input provides added convenience for any users who find it cumbersome to manually interact with small screens. Speech output will also be enabling, compared to text-only output, for visually impaired users. Users with motor impairments might be able to read text output, but might benefit from being able to respond verbally rather than using a keyboard or touchscreen. For users who are deaf or hard of hearing, however, a speech-only system creates barriers to usage.

The principle of "universal design" emerged in the 1990s from observations around developing technologies with accessibility in mind. When systems are designed and developed thoughtfully for people with disabilities, it turns out that they benefit many people with no known disabilities. Captioning audio material is one example. Although the initial impetus of captioning was to provide access for deaf and hard-of-hearing people, it is helpful in many other situations, as well, such as people watching videos in noisy settings, or non-native speakers who can read captions more easily than they understand spoken language, or older viewers with mild hearing loss.

These universal design principles apply to design of VUIs, as well. Early instances of voice-enabled travel reservation systems emphasized that some information is easily spoken (e.g., "I want to fly from New York to California on Tuesday night, leaving around 4 PM."). But when a set of flight options is available, most users prefer to see the range of options as text rather than listening to them. Multimodality is recommended. Some information we prefer to hear; other information we prefer to see.

But to ensure that a system is available for all people to use, we can't defer to only "preferred" modalities of some sets of users, or we will eliminate usage for others. The key message to extract here is that multimodality should ensure that all modalities are available at all times, and that designers should not make assumptions about how all users will prefer to access these systems.

There are a number of VUI design principles to keep in mind, to ensure that the broadest number of users can use a product or service. Many of these are recognizable as generally good design overall, and not unique to people with disabilities. But although failing to incorporate these design principles might merely annoy a general user, these oversights could become barriers to inclusion for users with disabilities. For example, there are a number of ways to reduce cognitive load for users. Designers can put important information first (or last), avoid long menu options, and not combine multiple ideas in a single question.[1]

A qualitative study we conducted with a number of users with disabilities highlights some key gaps in emerging VUI systems, along with some of their recommendations for creating more enabling VUIs:

- Users with hearing loss are concerned that VUI devices don't work well with nonstandard speech types (for example, users with speech impairments or the characteristics of "deaf speech.") The proliferation of devices requiring speech input creates barriers to access. These users are looking for an option to create personalized voice recognition models of nonstandard speech; i.e., ones that are trained from spoken data from this specific set of users and which learn from them over time.

---

1 See Deborah Dahl, "Voice Should Be User-Friendly—to All Users." SpeechTechMag.com, November 2015 (*http://bit.ly/2gSBa5W*)

- Deaf users commented that any audio feedback or information from VUIs is obviously not useful for them. One user stated that "Most designers seem to think everyone can both speak and hear and thus a pure voice interface is the best thing ever. Which could certainly be true for blind folks, just as a purely visual interface would be awful for them. Both should always be provided."

- VUI devices often don't have easy methods to indicate recognition errors, or to correct when there are recognition errors. One design remedy would be to ensure that there are multiple visual indicators of events, indicating "understood," "error," "please repeat," and so on.

- For visually or motor-impaired users, ensure that everything is possible through the voice UI. Don't also depend on LED indicators, or routing users to visual displays from a companion app. Multimodality should be a user's choice, and not a requirement.

Many of these principles apply to all users—we all have days when stress and lack of sleep impair our cognitive abilities, and we all grow older and lose some of our vision capabilities. Making text easy to read by looking at contrast, font size, and color saturation, and having good affordances, is simply good design.

Conclusion

This chapter introduced many of the key concepts when designing VUIs. Many of them are drawn from the IVR world, with key differences. Basic strategies, such as well-designed error behavior, implicit versus explicit confirmation, and design artifacts such as sample dialogs and flows, apply in both cases.

Typical VUI project deliverables include:

- Sample dialogs (you might want to include actual recordings, especially if using a voice talent)

- Flow diagram

- Prompt lists (if using voice talent or pregenerated text-to-speech)

- Screen mocks (if this is a multimodal app)

If working with an external customer, these design deliverables will communicate what the finished product will look like and allow the customer to review and provide feedback. It also provides a way for everyone to agree on the design before it's been implemented.

Some of the key design concepts covered in this chapter are:

- Confirmation strategies (how your users know they were understood)

- Whether your VUI should use command-and-control or a more conversational mode

- Error handling (because there will be errors and they need to be handled gracefully)

- Context (remembering what users have said, either in the same conversation or in prior ones)

- Handling ambiguous input

- Help and other universal commands

Designing for mobile can be both a richer experience as well as more complex. You'll need to make decisions about how to let your users know when and where they can speak, and when and where to use visual feedback. In many cases, there will be no human to back up your experience.

Enabling users to speak to their phones and devices opens up an entire world of experiences; whether it's looking up a piece of trivia during a dinner argument, asking a device to dim the lights, or managing the everyday tasks of your life, VUI can enhance them all.

[3]

Personas, Avatars, Actors, and Video Games

AN IMPORTANT DECISION THAT you should consider when designing voice user interfaces (VUIs) on mobile devices is whether your VUI should have a visual representation. This could take the form of a still image, a cartoon avatar, or even recorded video of an actor. In addition, there are nonhuman avatars in the form of other familiar shapes such as monsters, animals, robots, aliens, and so on. Finally, there are abstract visual responses a VUI can show, without using an avatar.

This chapter helps you to decide whether your VUI needs a visual component, and if it does, what the best design practices are. This chapter does not go deeply into details of how to create and animate an avatar; it focuses on how an avatar is used specifically within a VUI system.

In addition, this chapter covers persona design. All VUIs, regardless of whether they have a visual component such as an avatar, will still have a persona.

Personas

There is no such thing as a voice user interface with no personality.
COHEN, GIANGOLA, AND BALOGH, 2004

In *Voice User Interface Design*, Cohen, Giangola, and Balogh define persona as follows:

> "Persona" is defined as the role that we assume to display our conscious intentions to ourselves or other people. In the world of voice user interfaces, the term "persona" is used as a rough equivalent of "character," as in a character in a book or film. A more satisfying technical definition of persona is the standardized mental image of a personality or character that users infer from the application's voice and

language choices. For the purposes of the VUI industry, persona is a vehicle by which companies can brand a service or project a particular corporate image via speech.

Humans are wired to anthropomorphize. A photo of a bathtub with holes where the faucet used to be becomes a surprised face (Figure 3-1). We talk to our pets as if they were humans.

FIGURE 3-1.
Surprised bathtub
(photo by author)

Trust that your users will be doing the same thing with your VUI. Whether you intended them to do so, users will ascribe personality traits to it. The best strategy is to decide on the personality yourself, while designing, rather than leave it up to chance.

When you're using an avatar, it becomes even more crucial to think about the personality behind it. When you create a visual representation, people are even more likely to see personality traits. Begin with personality traits and then design the visuals to match. When thinking about personality, here are some questions to ask:

- Will you let the user ask questions about the system itself? (For example, "What's your favorite color?")

- How will you handle rudeness and vulgarity?

- Are you OK with breaking the illusion that your VUI is human?

Some virtual assistants, such as Cortana, let you access a log of everything they know about you to edit it. According to the *Business Insider* article "Why Microsoft Doesn't Want Its Digital Assistant, Cortana, to Sound Too Human,"[1] this "breaks the illusion that Cortana is a human, which is just fine by Microsoft, while also making it a more useful tool."

The personality of your VUI will affect its behavior across the board: how it asks questions, how it copes with errors, and how it provides assistance.

Cortana's writers spent a lot of time thinking about her personality:

> Our approach on personality includes defining a voice with an actual personality. This included writing a detailed personality and laying out how we wanted Cortana to be perceived. We used words like witty, confident, and loyal to describe how Cortana responds through voice, text, and animated character. We wrote an actual script based on this definition that is spoken by a trained voice actress with thousands of responses to questions that will have variability to make Cortana feel like it has an actual personality and isn't just programmed with robotic responses.[2]

Cortana's writers even have a strategy for dealing with the inevitable harassment that some users will give a female virtual assistant. As Cortana writer Deborah Harrison shared in an interview with this book's author:

> Our stance here is that we want to avoid turning anything resembling genuine harassment—sexual or otherwise—into a game. In lots of other scenarios, we write a variety of responses for any given query so that it's fun to ask more than once and so that we can explore different nuances of certain scenarios. And for some queries that are merely impertinent or rude or cheeky, we'll be more apt to respond with some cheekiness of our own. For example, if you say, "I hate you," Cortana might say, "Oh good, because I'm in opposite world right now!" Or

1   Weinberger, M. (2016). "Why Microsoft Doesn't Want Its Digital Assistant, Cortana, to Sound Too Human." Retrieved from *http://www.businessinsider.com/why-microsoft-doesnt-want-cortana-to-sound-too-human-2016-2/*.

2   Ash, M. (2015). "How Cortana Comes to Life in Windows 10." Retrieved from *http://blogs.windows.com/*.

she might say, "The feeling is not mutual." If you say, "You are boring," we'll give you any of several one-word answers like "Hooey!" or "Balderdash!" along with a picture of an animal that looks in some way affronted or surprised. So, she doesn't take offense just because you say something negative. But if you start saying things that have connotations of abuse, she stops playing and instead just states clearly that that's not a place where she'll engage. You could make the argument that she should just not respond at all, but that might feel unintelligent. She understands, but she's setting a boundary for herself—this isn't how she wants to be treated, and she'll say so, without rancor or anger, but firmly.

For other designers facing this conundrum, my advice would be to think carefully about the principles that are consistent with the personality you're developing. There are a variety of lenses you can apply: product goals, company goals, ethical goals, social goals, and so on. Each of these contributes to the cocktail of principles you develop. Those principles can evolve—should evolve, really—and grow to meet new scenarios, but having a core set of guidelines that define both what you intend to accomplish with your personality and how that looks helps guide the conversations when they arise. For example, this year we needed to figure out how to approach politics. How should Cortana respond when asked about a candidate? A policy? An election? We spent weeks discussing the nuances by looking through each of the lenses I listed above, and we ended up defining how Cortana feels about democracy, voting, candidacy, and political involvement. Now, as new queries arise that warrant attention, we have a set of principles to call on that help inform our approach. The writing still takes whatever time it takes, but we know how Cortana should sound.

Deciding how to approach abusive language is essential for any team undertaking this journey. Every digital assistant will face it.

On the flip side of persona design, make sure you don't go too over-board with personality traits when they're not needed. If you're design-ing an entertainment app, you may want to go full bore with witty dia-log and one-liners (á la, *You Don't Know Jack*), but imagine if Google suddenly began imbuing that kind of behavior into its virtual assistant. Consistency in your persona design is important: as Katherine Isbister and Clifford Nass note, "Consistency in others allows people to predict what will happen when they engage with them."[3]

If you're designing an app for a particular set of users, you can be more free with the personality. Some people won't like it, but some people will love it. If you're designing something more universal, be more cau-tious. In this case, you might have a subtler personality that is neither loved nor hated.

You might want to give your users choices for the avatar or voice used in your app. It is nice to give people options, but you can't always swap out an avatar or voice and leave everything else the same. Different looks and different voices imply different personalities, and the interactions different personalities have will not be identical. Ideally, rather than offering a different voice or different avatar, you offer different *perso-nas*, which then contain different components, including visual and audio. Having a mismatched persona and avatar can cause inconsisten-cies and lead to distrust.

The book *Voice User Interface Design* by Cohen, Giangola, and Balogh is a great reference for learning more about persona and VUIs.

Should My VUI Be Seen?

One of the most common use cases for which designers do create ava-tars is virtual assistants. Websites often use a photo or an avatar (Figure 3-2) for their customer service chatbot (even those who do not speak and cannot be spoken to). Many mobile virtual assistants also have an avatar component.

---

3 Isbister, K., and Nass, C. "Consistency of Personality in Interactive Characters: Verbal Cues, Non-Verbal Cues, and User Characteristics." *International Journal of Human–Computer Studies* 53 (2000): 251–267.

FIGURE 3-2.

Examples of websites with an avatar (left, Jetstar—not animated; right, CodeBaby—animated)

However, many of the most prominent VUI assistants, including Google, Siri, Hound, and Cortana, have no avatar. Some do have simple visual cues, such as a glowing circle. (HAL 9000, a fictitious but very interactive virtual assistant from the 1968 movie *2001: A Space Odyssey*, had a glowing red light.) Avatars are *not* essential to have a successful voice interaction. VUIs can still provide empathy and important visual feedback without using a picture.

The designers of Cortana made a conscious decision to stay away from an anthropomorphic representation. Deborah Harrison, Cortana editorial writer at Microsoft, says:

> One reason we stayed away from a human-looking avatar is that we're clear that Cortana isn't human. It was more true to her nature to show her as a more purely digital representation.

A good avatar takes more work, both on the design and development. There are third parties out there that will provide an avatar for you to integrate with, or you can invest in building your own.

Using an Avatar: What *Not to* Do

In "Sweet Talking Your Computer," Clifford Nass notes:

> Clippy's problem was that he was utterly oblivious to the appropriate ways to treat people. Every time a user typed "Dear..." Clippy would dutifully propose, "I see you are writing a letter. Would you like some help?"—no matter how many times the user had rejected this offer in the past. Clippy never learned anyone's names or preferences. If you think of Clippy as a person, of course he would evoke hatred and scorn.[4]

Microsoft's assistant, Clippy, was a failure, but it came with some important lessons. Clippy (Figure 3-3) was oblivious to context. In one cartoon making fun of Clippy, someone has started a letter with "Dear World, I just can't take it any more" and Clippy has popped up to say "It looks like you're writing a suicide letter. Let me help with that."

FIGURE 3-3.
Microsoft Office assistant, Clippy

---

4 Nass, C. (2010). "Sweet Talking Your Computer: Why People Treat Devices Like Humans; Saying Nice Things to a Machine to Protect its 'Feelings.'" Retrieved from *http://wsj.com/.*

If your VUI is tone-deaf, the user will notice. Another Nass experiment had subjects "drive" a car simulator and used two different voices: one that was upbeat, and one that was morose. Sad drivers hearing the happy voice had approximately twice as many accidents as those who heard the sad voice. Happy drivers had fewer accidents and paid more attention to the road when they heard the happy voice. When voices matched mood, drivers also reported enjoying driving more and that they liked the voice more.

If your app is just looking up search results and setting timers, emotional tone is not as important. But if the app deals with more sensitive topics such as mood or health, be sure to recognize these instances and handle them appropriately. It's better to have a neutral response than to have one that is inappropriately happy or sad. Making your VUI appear *aware* of what the user has said (or done) is crucial.

In a study done by Ann Thyme-Gobbel during her time as head of UX/UI experience and design at healthcare company 22otters (and presented at the Mobile Voice 2016 conference), 72 participants were shown a video with the same instruction done in one of five ways (Figure 3-4 shows some of these):

- Static photo

- Animated avatar

- Static picture of same avatar

- Text only

- Animated illustration (not an avatar)

FIGURE 3-4.
Photo, static avatar, illustration

Participants heard the same prompts (recorded by a person, not text-to-speech) delivered in one of those formats, and then were asked which one they preferred. Generally speaking, most people preferred the animated illustration. When asked specifically what they thought of the moving avatar, those over the age of 40 rated it the highest.

Subjects appreciated variation—text, for example, is great for listing medications; illustrations are useful for instructions on using a device; and avatars are good for building rapport.

The study began with a static avatar introducing each topic, which as Thyme-Gobbel said, "grounded the voice and made a nice connector throughout the app."

Though it was a small study, it's a reminder that avatars are not appropriate all the time. Whenever possible, prototype your VUI early on to discover in advance whether people find your avatar engaging—or creepy.

Using an Avatar (or Recorded Video): What *to* Do

When should you use an avatar? This section outlines where an avatar or animated character can enhance your VUI and keep users more engaged.

Storytelling

A great time to use an avatar/character is for storytelling and engagement. If you want to draw your user into your world, whether it's for a game, or for educational purposes, having a character is a great way to do so.

An example of this is from the ToyTalk children's entertainment app SpeakaZoo. In each scene, an animated animal talks to the child, and when it's the child's turn to talk, a microphone button lights up (Figure 3-5).

FIGURE 3-5.

ToyTalk's SpeakaZoo

Based on the child's responses, the animated character responds in different ways. In this instance, the app does not even use that much speech recognition—it often reacts the same regardless of what the child says. It still creates an immersive experience, although with repeated exposure, kids do catch on that the character is always doing or saying the same thing.

Another example of an interactive game with an avatar is Merly, from Botanic.io (Figure 3-6). Mark Stephen Meadows describes Merly as follows:

> Merly, a character that provides backstory on a kid's mystery fable, answered questions that the story brought up, provided solutions on how to play the game, and stitched together several elements of the story that were not clear on first read. It was a new way to read, and someone that, like the Greek chorus in plays, added meta-commentary by breaking the fourth wall. Narrative bots have to break that fourth wall and what that means, from an interactive narrative point of view, is that they will be an increasingly important part of storytelling as VR eclipses passive narrative media like movies and television.

FIGURE 3-6.
Merly from Botanic.io

Teamwork

Another way an avatar can add to your user's experience is that it allows the user to have a teammate/collaborator when completing tasks. When you speak to Amazon Echo's Alexa, for example, she's the one completing the task; you're making a request.

With an avatar, the VUI can be a separate entity from the system or the company with which the user is interacting. For example, if your doctor has requested that you take your blood pressure every day, a nurse avatar can assist you with that, so *together* you accomplish the required task someone else has requested.

SILVIA's Gracie prototype of an avatar (Figure 3-7) allows the user to sing along with her (she's an animated character). When you want to talk to Gracie, you tap the screen.

FIGURE 3-7.
Gracie lets you sing
along with her

Gracie will continue to say things to you even when you haven't tapped the screen, which adds to the feeling you're having a real conversation.

Video Games

Video games are another format in which VUIs can enhance the user's immersion in the virtual experience; however, it must be done well.

Some video games use voice to allow the player to issue commands. For example, in Yakuza Studio's third-person shooter game *Binary Domain* you can issue commands to your team such as "Cover me!", "Regroup!", and "Fire!"—and they might or might not do it, depending on whether they like you (Figure 3-8). Although you're allowed to speak and issue these commands at any time during game play, at certain points characters ask you questions, and show options on the screen.

FIGURE 3-8.
Voice options in *Binary Domain*

If the system did not understand you, you'll hear, "Don't get ya. Tell me later."

Another game, *In Verbis Virtus* by Indomitus Games, uses speech recognition to empower the user to cast spells. For example, the user can say, "Let there be light!" and the screen will light up (Figure 3-9).

FIGURE 3-9.
Casting spells via voice in the game *In Verbis Virtus*

An interesting twist is that the spells are in a made-up language called Maha'ki, making it even more immersive, since it feels like you're speaking a magical language. Many users report really enjoying this feature of the game.

There Came an Echo, by Iridium Studios, is a strategy game that allows you to control your team of four via voice commands (Figure 3-10). One nice feature is that you can set up your own aliases; for example, you could substitute "burn it down" for "fire when ready." You can even call characters by other names of your choice. It allows you to choose your mode: push to talk, or "always listening". The commands you issued show up on the screen, as well, so you can keep track of how you've been directing your team. Characters respond to your commands with "Yes, sir" and "You got it," adding an element of realism (as well as letting you know it worked).

FIGURE 3-10.
Voice commands in *There Came an Echo* are listed in the upper-right corner

There Came an Echo has mixed reviews, but users seem to feel the voice command is what makes it a better game. Here's a YouTube review by a user named TotalBiscuit (emphasis added by this book's author):

> The voice command really is the key factor for this particular title...It's the voice command that gives it the pacing, and it's the voice command that makes it challenging, because everything's being done in real time and it requires you to think on your feet quite rapidly. Not to mention there is a serious amount of cool factor involved in the voice command...**This one does it really well because I think it sticks**

within its means. It doesn't go overboard with the voice commands. It doesn't use too many of them, and it limits what you can do to the point where the voice commands are accurate and they're going to be quick & responsive...The game does not play anywhere near as well without it...This game is more than the sum of its parts thanks to the voice command system.

Most of these games have a calibration setting to help improve accuracy (Figure 3-11). *Binary Domain,* for example, asks the user to run through various phrases and gives it a score to let the user know how well they can expect performance of speech recognition during game play.

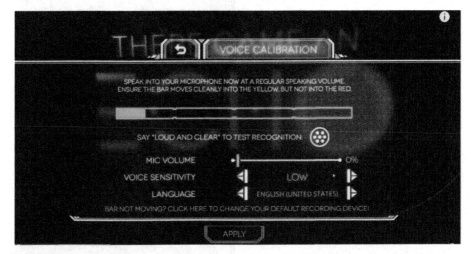

FIGURE 3-11.
Voice calibration setting in *There Came an Echo*

Another unique example of adding VUI to a video game was 2008's *Eagle Eye Freefall,* a short interactive experience that went along with the release of the movie *Eagle Eye.* The game was developed by Telefon Projekt, and the experience began when the user entered their phone number on the game's website. Shortly thereafter, the user would receive a phone call on their actual phone, and a mysterious voice would direct the user to follow instructions on their computer and speak to different characters over the phone.

When Should I Use Video in My VUI?

There are very few examples of VUI apps out there right now that use real human actors for having interactive conversations. Using real faces can be an extremely engaging way to involve users, but it is also a much more expensive endeavor.

At Volio, we created interactive conversations in which the majority of the screen on a mobile device was filled by the actor's face, along with a small picture-in-picture element that displayed the user (Figure 3-12).

FIGURE 3-12.
Volio app, "Talk to Ron"

Having the screen mostly taken up by the actor's face made the experience very personal and one-on-one for users. Users naturally responded via voice to the actor, with no instructions. Despite knowing the content was not live, many users reported feeling as though they were engaged in a real conversation with the person on the screen.

Technically, however, creating these types of interactions takes a lot of planning. It requires a studio with professional lighting, and for each take, the actor must look the same and have the same head position. This makes it very difficult to add or fix content later; even if you can rebook the actor, replicating the exact lighting, appearance, and head position is challenging.

Adding VUI to prerecorded video only makes sense if the VUI part is also a rich experience. Another example of a video app had a sports celebrity who answered questions. After he spoke, he would end with a question such as "What do you want me to tell you more about?" A screen would then pop up to the let user know what they could say; for example, "Say SPORTS or OFF THE FIELD." At this point, the user would press the microphone button and say one of those items.

Allowing the user to speak one of these choices did not add to the intimacy of the experience; it was clunky, not conversational. The same could have easily been accomplished by pressing buttons.

Visual VUI—Best Practices

Now that we've run through some examples of when it's a good idea—or not a good idea—to use an avatar/character/actor in your VUI, let's get into some of the best practices for when you *do* use one.

Should My Users See Themselves?

In some cases, allowing the user to see herself talking back can provide more engagement. You are probably familiar with the FaceTime model, in which the person you're speaking with takes up the majority of the screen, and there is a small rectangle showing your face, as well.

A clever example of this in a storytelling context is in the ToyTalk app *The Winston Show.* In one scene, Winston appears on the bridge of a spaceship and announces he's just discovered an alien lifeform. He asks his shipmate to put the alien "on screen"—and there is the face of the child using the app (Figure 3-13).

We used the picture-in-picture model in our Volio apps, as well, which was generally a familiar-feeling element because of user's experience with FaceTime, Skype, and so on. Occasionally users said they preferred not to see themselves on the screen, however, so it is worth considering making this a user-controlled feature.

FIGURE 3-13.
Example of an alien lifeform, aka the author's son

What About the GUI?

Another key question is whether your avatar or recorded video will have any graphical controls. With mobile devices, allowing the choice of speaking or using a graphical user interface (GUI) lets users decide how they want to respond. (Note: this is dependent on the type of experience you're designing. In the Volio case, UI elements were not shown unless the user was struggling, because we wanted to remain as much as possible in the speaking world, to keep the user engaged.)

Figure 3-14 shows an example of an avatar interaction in which the user can speak or press a button to respond.

When designing a multimodal app (one that has VUI and GUI), normal VUI timeouts are not applicable: if your user decides to press a button and not speak, it doesn't make sense for the avatar to suddenly say, "I'm sorry, I didn't get that," while the user is mulling over their choice of which button to push. In this case, treat it the same way you would if it were GUI-only: let the user have as much time as they want to either speak or press a button.

FIGURE 3-14.

In the case of GUI responses, the Sensely app allows the user to talk or tap

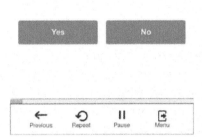

Is this for an urgent issue?

That being said, take note of places in your app where the user does not answer for a long time; there could be an underlying issue that's causing confusion, or perhaps reluctance for the user to respond.

Additionally, GUI controls do not make sense for all interactions. For example, if you have an open-ended question (such as "How are you feeling?") and you want to encourage your users to speak naturally, don't put in a list of possible responses. An additional case is when there is a very long list, such as "Which song would you like to hear?" Let the user first attempt to respond via voice/natural language; after a couple of failures, provide them with a way to select an answer or type one in.

Handling Errors

Speaking of errors, as always, don't forget to handle these cases in your VUI!

Having an avatar or video can allow for more interesting and clever responses when things go wrong. For example, in the Volio app with a stand-up comic named Robbie, a sample no-match response would show Robbie looking down and saying, "My bad...just looking at my phone and didn't hear you. When did you say you got married?" It takes the design principle of blaming the system to a whole new level.

An avatar or video also injects another important element for human conversational cues: eye gaze. If you are having a conversation with someone and they turn away, you know they're no longer paying attention. Your avatar can do the same. This worked well in the Volio case to indicate when the user has not been heard or understood; the first couple of times this occurred, rather than stopping and saying, "I didn't understand," the actor continued to simply look and listen. With no instruction, users naturally repeated themselves and quite often continued on successfully.

During filming, when the actors finished speaking, they would continue for 30 to 60 seconds of "active listening," which could then be played on a loop. The listening should not be exaggerated; all that's needed is to continue to look straight ahead, with the occasional nod or head movement. This nonverbal reminder gave the user the understanding that the system was continuing to listen, with no verbal or other reminders.

ToyTalk's *The Winston Show* allows the avatar to help the child learn how to interact. To speak, it requires the user to press and hold down the button while speaking (unlike most phone apps, which require the user to press once and then speak). If the user presses and releases right away, the animated character, Winston, says, "Oopsy, hold down the microphone!"

I assume that ToyTalk chose this model because very young children are not as likely to succeed with just push-to-talk; having them physically hold down the microphone button (or at least, hold their finger on the screen) reminds them that they are in a mode in which the app is expecting them to speak. It also means less reliance on endpoint detection.

Turn Taking and Barge-In

In a traditional interactive voice response (IVR) system, callers can typically "barge in" (interrupt) during prompt playback. This is very useful in an IVR system because users cannot easily skip ahead and don't want to hear all the available options before getting on with their tasks. In an IVR system, when a caller barges in, the prompt can be stopped, and after the user speaks again (or after a no-speech timeout) a new prompt can be played.

Allowing a user to barge in during a video is a tricky business. It will be jarring to switch to a new video, presumably one of the actor just listening. For these systems, it is advisable to turn off barge-in because it will be too challenging to handle the interruption from a technical standpoint.

However, because this system is human-like, people do not tend to interrupt, because they're waiting for their turn to speak—they're not waiting to issue a command. Your video VUI is unlikely to be droning on about a list of menu options (and if it does, you should revisit your decision to use a recording of an actor in the first place).

Fine-tuning the point at which a user can begin speaking, however, is crucial. It's essential to turn listening on at the exact second (or millisecond) the actor (or avatar) finishes speaking because this is when the user is most likely to speak. If the first second or two of their utterance is not captured, they are more likely to be misunderstood. It is also essential to let the user know *when* they can speak, such as highlighting the border around their face (if you're implementing picture-in-picture) in green, or another type of visual indicator. In this model, in which the user can simply speak without pressing a button, a microphone icon is not necessarily the right indicator, because users might try to press it. Animating the microphone can help. It's best to test your visual indicator thoroughly with real users to see what works.

In summary, this type of conversational style, in which the video and the user take turns speaking, needs to have multiple components:

- No barge-in.
- After the actor is finished speaking, they continue in "active listening" mode.
- A visual indicator that it's the user's turn to speak.
- A prompt makes it obvious that it's the user's turn (e.g., asks a question, or command, such as "Please tell me more about that.").
- The system begins listening immediately after the actor finishes speaking.

These apply for avatars, as well.

In the avatar world, there might be cases in which these conventions are not followed. For ToyTalk's animated apps, the microphone icon displays an "X" to indicate when speaking is not allowed. When it's the child's turn to talk, the microphone lights up and flashes.

Because these are (a) used by young children and (b) more of a story-telling mode than a back-and-forth conversation, it's necessary to let the child know when they should speak. Barge-in would not work well here at all, because young kids will often be talking along with the app and it would interrupt the story to stop whenever the system thought it heard something.

There are other cases for which requiring the user to "push to talk" are useful, as well. With a virtual assistant, you might not expect users to have a set conversation every time (such as with some entertainment or health apps). It could be more of a short series of back-and-forths, during which the user is trying to complete a task or get information, and it's important to allow the user to interrupt. For example, if the user asks for a list of nearby coffee houses with WiFi, the app will produce a list; it's not yet clear if the user will continue to speak (perhaps by saying, "Which ones are open until 10 PM?") or whether the user's request has been satisfied.

In this example, it is very important to *allow* the user to continue the conversation, but don't automatically turn the microphone back on—let the user control the conversational pace. This is the methodology used for most of the current virtual assistants out there (Siri, Google, Hound, and Cortana).

Maintaining Engagement and the Illusion of Awareness

Regardless of whether your VUI uses an avatar/video, keeping your users engaged is paramount.

What are the best ways to create and maintain the illusion of awareness? Some great tips come from the creators of the trivia game *You Don't Know Jack* (Figure 3-15). Originally released in the late 1990s as a PC game, *You Don't Know Jack* later won both the Most Innovative Interface and Best Overall Interface at Apple Computer's distinguished Human Interface Design Excellence Awards.

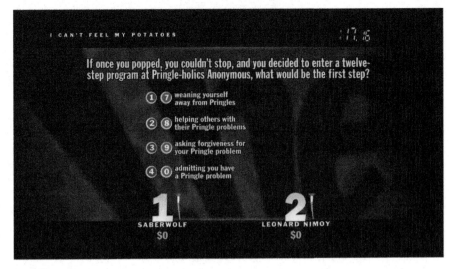

FIGURE 3-15.
You Don't Know Jack trivia game

It does not use speech recognition, but the game does an amazing job of sucking users in as if they were playing a live game show with a live host. It does this with all prerecorded content.

Harry Gottlieb, the game's creator, wrote "The Jack Principles of the Interactive Conversation Interface" in 2002. In his paper, Gottlieb outlines tips for creating the illusion of awareness in a conversational system; specifically, he suggests responding with human intelligence and emotion to the following:

- The user's actions
- The user's inactions
- The user's past actions
- A series of the user's actions
- The actual time and space that the user is in
- The comparison of different users' situations and actions

How can you accomplish this? As mentioned in Chapter 2, keeping track of the past is very important. If the user has just requested information about primatologist Jane Goodall, and then she follows-up with the question, "Where did she go to college?" don't act like you don't know who the user is talking about.

Avatars can even react to a user's inactions or to errors. If a user hasn't spoken at a point in the game when they're expected to, the avatar could cross its arms, tap its foot, or say, "I'm waiiiting!"

By using an avatar or actor, you can help maintain the illusion of awareness even more. An example of this was used in a Volio app that allowed the user to have a conversation with a stand-up comedian. If it was morning, the actor would say, "What are you doing up so early?" to start the conversation. If the time of day is relevant, use that information. Don't offer to transfer the user to an agent if it's outside of business hours. Use information about the time to make it more real.

In "Jack Principles" Gottlieb also outlined tips for *maintaining* the illusion of awareness:

- Use dialog that conveys a sense of intimacy

- Ensure that characters act appropriately while the user is interacting

- Ensure that dialog never seems to repeat

- Be aware of the number of simultaneous users

- Be aware of the gender of the users

- Ensure that the performance of the dialog is seamless

- Avoid the presence of characters when user input cannot be evaluated

Another way to build trust with an avatar is to follow human conversational conventions when appropriate. For example, when users call to speak with a call center agent, they don't usually launch into a full description of the problem. Here's an example of a nonstandard interaction:

AGENT
Hi, thanks for calling Acme Cable Company.

CALLER
It says on my bill I owe $5.99 for something called federal tax, and I've never seen that before and I want you to take it off.

Instead, the agent tries to establish some initial rapport and ease the caller into the conversation, building up trust:

AGENT
Hi, thanks for calling Acme Cable Company. How are you doing today?

CALLER
I'm good, how are you?

AGENT
I'm fine, thanks. What can I help you with today?

CALLER
I have a question about my bill.

AGENT
OK, I can help you with that. What seems to be the issue?

CALLER
Yeah, well, there is a charge for $5.99 I don't understand...

Notice how the agent begins with a question unrelated to the cable company: the "How are you doing?" question. Then, when the agent asks how she can help, the caller breaks it into pieces—first, the general topic ("my bill") and then the specifics. You can do the same thing with your VUI system, if you plan to have a conversation.

People often like to tell their stories via a narrative. When people go to the doctor, they don't usually give all the details right up front about what's wrong; instead, they give one piece at a time. I've witnessed this at nurse advisor call centers. I have seen good results with this approach using an avatar, as well. Expecting the user to always throw out all the details of their question or issue right off the bat will often result in not understanding; instead, break it into normal conversational snippets.

Think carefully about the beginning of your conversations. As an example, at Sensely, we sometimes begin with a general "How are you doing?" This gets the conversational ball rolling—people often respond with a simple, "I'm fine, thanks," but sometimes go into more detail. If you choose to utilize this technique, you'll need to be able to handle both types of responses.

Visual (Non-Avatar) Feedback

Avatars and actors are not the only kind of visual feedback your VUI can have. You can use visual feedback to let the user know when your VUI is listening, when it's thinking, or when it didn't understand. Some virtual assistants, like Cortana, go further (Figure 3-16).

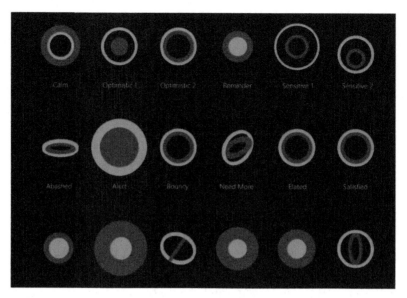

FIGURE 3-16.
The many moods of Cortana (*http://genieblog.ch/*)

Here's how one designer at Microsoft describes designing Cortana's visual "moods":

> One of the things we debated quite a bit during the planning process was our decision to include an actual shape to embody Cortana. We explored a variety of concepts ranging from using colors on notifications to simple geometric shapes to a full-blown, human-like avatar. In the end, we worked with the creative team at 343 (the studio that develops Halo!) and landed on something we think makes Cortana feel more alive than if we just used a voice. Cortana is programmed to respond to different questions and present different answers based on the grid of emotions and states below. If Cortana correctly answers your question and is happy, Cortana will let you know. If Cortana can't understand you, there will be slight embarrassment.[5]

---

5   Ash, M. (2015). "How Cortana Comes to Life in Windows 10." Retrieved from *http://blogs.windows.com/*.

Do the variants on the blue circles work? I doubt users, if shown each circle out of context, could name what emotion or task Cortana was engaged in at that time. However, over time, it's quite likely users would come to associate them subconsciously. People are very good at patterns and will be quick to pick up on common ones such as the "listening" icon.

As shown in Figure 3-17, the Amazon Echo—a device rather than a mobile app—uses blue lights on the top of its cylinder to let you know when it's listening (after you say the wake word, "Alexa"). This is a subtle but useful way to let users know that they can speak. After about five seconds, if Alexa does not hear anything, the light disappears.

FIGURE 3-17.
Amazon Echo has a blue ring that lights up to indicate when the user should speak

On the other hand, if you say something that Alexa was completely unable to process, the light pattern changes, and an "end" sound plays, letting you know Alexa *did* hear you, but was not able to understand. This is particularly useful if you're talking to it from another room or not facing it. There is one more response for not understanding, which is when Alexa is pretty sure you made a request or asked a question but could not understand it or fulfill it, in which case another light pattern is shown, and she says something along the lines of, "Hmm, I can't find the answer to the question I heard."

Jibo, billed as a "family robot," has a lot of personality without appearing human (Figure 3-18). It's a small cylinder with a rounded top on a swivel base. Its "face" is a screen that can have animations such as a heart.

FIGURE 3-18.

The Jibo robot

Jibo can respond to voice commands and uses text-to-speech (TTS) to generate spoken responses. Jibo is designed to evoke an emotional response from the user. A review in online magazine *Mashable* states, "Jibo isn't an appliance, it's a companion, one that can interact and react with its human owners in ways that delight."[6]

But a word of caution also applies: Jibo definitely evokes emotion, but is it appropriate in all situations? For example, can it be serious enough to serve as a health advisor?

Choosing a Voice

Choosing a voice for your VUI is another important consideration. Will you use TTS or recorded prompts? The voice is a crucial aspect of your design:

> First, designers should cast voices base on more than clarity and tonal quality. They should also attend to the consistency of voices with the behaviors, attitudes, and language of the character or agent to which it will be attached. This will likely require more than instinct. Voices need

---

6 *http://on.mash.to/2fQwQiE*

to be evaluated by users so that consistency can be coordinated and verified... Also, a badly cast voice is likely much worse than no voice at all. Voices will have social meaning, whether it is wanted or not.[7]

Chapter 5 goes more into detail about this topic.

Pros of an Avatar

To summarize, let's look at the pros and cons of using an avatar. This should help guide your decision about whether to use one for your VUI.

Let's begin with the advantages of having an avatar as part of your VUI. First, avatars can offer more engagement with the user.

In a study conducted at the University of Southern California's Institute for Creative Technologies, subjects were asked to respond to a series of questions such as "How old are you?" and "What makes you happy?" There were three groups: an animated virtual human, a still picture of a virtual human, and an audio-only version.

There were 24 questions in all, and the subjects were told they had to answer at least 12 questions and had the option of answering all 24. The number of subjects who answered all 24 questions was much higher in the case for which the questions were asked by the animated virtual human. In addition, on average, people's responses were longer when answering the animated virtual human.

Another USC ICT study had subjects speak with a virtual assistant who helped people suffering from post-traumatic stress disorder (PTSD) after military service. Subjects reported feeling more comfortable disclosing information to the virtual assistant than to a human, possibly because the virtual assistant was less critical.

I have seen a similar effect at Sensely, which uses a virtual nurse to help people with chronic health conditions. Patients often open up to the avatar and tell her when they're feeling stressed or about other health conditions.

---

7   Nass, C., and Reeves, B. *The Media Equation*. (Stanford, CA: CSLI Publications, 1996), 177.

Even simple faces can evoke emotional responses; "a few lines depicting a 'smiley face' can lead people to feel sadness, surprise, or anger with a change in one or two strokes of a pen.[8] In addition, "although people can certainly listen without seeing a speaker's face, they have a clear and strong bias toward the integration of faces and voices."[9] Everyone reads lips to a degree; it's more difficult to understand someone when you can't see his or her mouth.

Mark Stephen Meadows, president of avatar company Botanic, has this to say about when we should use an avatar:

> When should we meet in person, and when can we just talk on the phone? We talk on the phone all the time and we can get along just fine with only voice. But most of us, at least when we have the time, prefer face-to-face meetings. We get more information. It's more fun, we get more done, there's less misunderstanding, and it builds cool human things like trust and empathy. So, it's really dependent on the use case, the user, and specifics.

He calls avatars the GUI of the VUI. Meadows reminds us of another thing avatars provide—additional clues to personality that will tell us how to interface with them:

> Go visit a hospital, hotel, or restaurant and you'll see that the employees have specific personalities, or roles, that they play out. This is important because we need to know how to interact with whom, and so these employees dress in particular ways and act in a particular fashion to frame the interaction. If you visit a hotel, hospital, airport, or some other service-oriented place of business, you can observe these ontologies. They even have hierarchies of power that are reflected in how they act and dress. In hotels, we meet the receptionist, manager, and housekeeper. In airports, we meet attendants, pilots, and mechanics. In restaurants, it's the hostess, chef, and dishwasher. And in hospitals, we meet the receptionist, doctor, and janitor. These personalities frame the experience and interaction. So, I don't care if there's a GUI or not, but virtual assistants need personality so we know how to interface with them. These personalities are reflected in their appearance.

---

8   Nass, C., and Reeves, B. *The Media Equation.* (Stanford, CA: CSLI Publications, 1996), 177.

9   Nass, C., and Brave, S. *Wired for Speech.* (Cambridge, MA: The MIT Press, 2005), 176–177.

The manager, pilot, chef, and doctor all dress in a particular way so we know who they are. These are archetypes, and avatars should be designed with that stuff in mind.

Users anthropomorphize computers, even without an avatar face. We take what we know about our interactions with humans and apply them. As Clifford Nass says:

> People respond to computers and other technologies using the same social rules and expectations that they use when interacting with other people. These responses are not spur-of-the-moment reactions. They run broadly and deeply.[10]

People often extend politeness to computers, as well, as evidenced by an experiment Nass ran at Stanford:

> After being tutored by a computer, half of the participants were asked about the computer's performance by the computer itself, and the other half were asked by an identical computer across the room. Remarkably, the participants gave significantly more positive responses to the computer that asked about itself than they did to the computer across the room. These weren't overly sensitive people: They were graduate students in computer science and electrical engineering, all of whom insisted that they would never be polite to a computer.

If you are designing a system in which you need a high level of engagement, such as for healthcare or entertainment, consider an avatar, or at least a face.

For tasks with less of an emotional component, such as scheduling meetings, choosing a movie, making a shopping list, or doing a search query, an avatar might not be necessary and could even be a distraction.

The Downsides of an Avatar

Now that we've seen some of the advantages of using an avatar, let's look at the other side.

---

10 Nass, C. (2010). "Sweet Talking Your Computer: Why People Treat Devices Like Humans; Saying Nice Things to a Machine to Protect its 'Feelings.'" Retrieved from *http://wsj.com/*.

Avatars do take a lot of extra work, and if they're not done well, they can annoy or put off your users. Avatars that merely blink but show no emotional reaction or awareness can be more of a hindrance than an asset.

As of this writing, the majority of avatars in the virtual assistant space are female, usually young and sexy. Unless you're writing a virtual assistant for an adult entertainment app, there's no reason for this. I recently downloaded a virtual assistant that had a young attractive cartoon woman as the default avatar. She doesn't do anything besides occasionally blink (or wink). The app allows you to choose different avatars, and the list that came up was a series of scantily-clad women. Plus, a dog.

If you have an avatar, spend time deciding on who it will be. Don't just let your user pick one at random. Begin with the avatar's top personality traits. Should the avatar be more authoritative or more caring? Professional? Knowledgeable? Create the *persona* first, and design the avatar that speaks to those qualities. Persona is not just about looks; it influences how your VUI speaks and responds. If the image of the VUI changes, the persona and prompts should change, as well. If your VUI has an avatar, another set of questions will need to be answered: how much of the avatar will be shown: just the face? The face and upper body? The entire body? Will it be two-dimensional or three-dimensional? How many emotional expressions can be shown? How will the lip synching be done? Will your avatar occupy the entire screen or just a part of it? All of these things influence how your users will respond and interact with your VUI.

One thing to keep in mind when designing your avatar is that a very strong personality can have a negative effect. As Thyme-Gobbel says, "the stronger its persona, the more polarized the user reaction."

You might have people who love it and some who hate it. You might have users who love having an avatar, and others who do not. Depending on your app, that might be OK—sometimes it's best to not design for everyone; instead, you might find it advantageous to design for a particular user group that might appreciate that "strong" personality. For example, fans of a particular video game might love an avatar that is "in character" and demonstrates that character's personality traits. On the other hand, an avatar that's supposed to be a personal assistant for a whole host of user groups should tone down some of the more extreme traits.

In addition, don't make assumptions about what your user will want. For example, don't assume that everyone wants a female avatar over a male avatar. As always, do as much user testing as possible with your avatar choice and prompts. If your avatar is *too* gimmicky—for example, using a lot of slang—it might make it more difficult to predict what the user will say back.

The Uncanny Valley

Another thing to be aware of when designing an avatar is not to fall into the *uncanny valley*. The uncanny valley refers to the shudder of horror you feel when you see something that is very close to being human—but not quite. Figure 3-19 shows the dip into the uncanny valley—for example, a zombie is at the bottom of the valley and very disturbing to us.

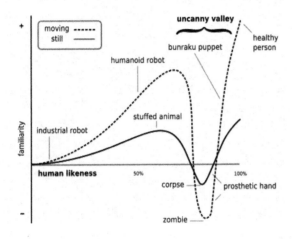

FIGURE 3-19.
The uncanny valley[11]

One way to avoid the uncanny valley is to make the avatar not photorealistic, or make it nonhuman (such as an animal).

---

11 By Smurrayinchester: self-made, based on image by Masahiro Mori and Karl MacDorman at *http://www.androidscience.com/theuncannyvalley/proceedings2005/uncannyvalley.html*, CC BY-SA 3.0, *https://commons.wikimedia.org/w/index.php?curid=2041097.*

As Meadows points out, having a recorded human voice with a cartoon doesn't trip our "uncanny valley" sensors: just think about Pixar movies.

It's important to match the avatar's expressions with the words and emotions it is expressing, or it can be very jarring and unpleasant. An example of this can be seen in a conversation with a robot named Sophia. She has just said, "I feel like I could be a good partner to humans. An ambassador," but at the end of that sentence, her lip curls into a sneer (Figure 3-20). It makes one doubt the sincerity of her words—a worse outcome than having no expression at all. As Nass says, "Facial expression needs to match what is said, or people perceive an attempt at deception."[12]

FIGURE 3-20.
Sophia by Hanson Robotics—why the sneer?

Conclusion

Spend time deciding whether your VUI will have a visual component. Don't just add an avatar because it's cool. Is your system conversational? Entertaining? Empathetic? These are better candidates for an avatar or actor.

---

12 Nass, C., and Brave, S. *Wired for Speech.* (Cambridge, MA: The MIT Press, 2005), 181.

Investing in an avatar is not a small task. To build your own avatar, you'll need a design team just for that piece, or you can use avatars made by third parties. Having your avatar show emotion, without looking creepy or repeating the same gestures over and over, is challenging. Think carefully about why you want to use an avatar, and do user testing on prototypes to make sure you're on the right path.

Using a real actor can be an incredibly engaging experience, but this comes with a cost, as well: because everything must be filmed in a studio, you really need to get it right the first time.

A virtual assistant can still be very successful, even without a face. Do take advantage of other types of visual feedback, however, to let the user know when the system is listening or doesn't understand.

[4]

Speech Recognition Technology

WE'VE TALKED ABOUT MANY of the crucial voice user interface (VUI) design elements. So far, they've been light on the technical details of speech recognition technology itself. This chapter gets more technical, looking under the hood so that you can make sure your VUI design takes into account (and takes advantage of) the technology itself. It will also give you the ability to confidently reference the underlying technology when explaining your design decisions.

To create a VUI, your app must have one key component: automated speech recognition (ASR). ASR refers to the technology by which a user speaks, and their speech is then translated into text.

Choosing an Engine

So how to choose your ASR tool? There are free services as well as those that require licensing fees. Some offer free use for development but require payment for commercial use.

As of this writing, there are two major fee-based speech recognition engines: Google and Nuance. Other options in this space include Microsoft's Bing and iSpeech.

Free ASR tools include the Web Speech API, Wit.ai, Sphinx (from Carnegie Mellon), and Kaldi. Amazon has its own tool, but at the moment it can be used only when creating skills for the Amazon Echo (which is free).

Wikipedia has a much more detailed list, which you can access at *https://en.wikipedia.org/wiki/List_of_speech_recognition_software.*

Some companies offer multiple engines, as well; for example, Nuance has different offerings depending on what you plan to do, such as a medical app or dictation.

When choosing an engine, there are two things that are key:

- Robustness of dataset/accuracy

- Endpoint detection performance

New companies often have difficulty breaking into the speech recognition market—they might have good technology, they simply don't have the data that larger companies have spent years amassing. Therefore, their recognition will probably not be as good, depending on how wide the domain is.

Often, people become so caught up in focusing on an ASR tool's accuracy that they forget about the second crucial requirement: good *endpoint detection*. Endpoint detection is a fancy way of describing how the computer knows when you begin and finish speaking. Choosing an engine with good endpoint (or end-of-speech) detection is crucial. I'll get into that a little bit later in this chapter.

It can be tempting to use the cheapest available ASR tool in your design, but beware: if the recognition accuracy is poor, or the endpoint detection is sloppy, your user experience will suffer greatly. Having "pretty good" recognition might seem good enough, but users will quickly grow frustrated and give up on your product.

It is also worth noting that not all ASR tools include important advanced features like *N*-best lists, settable parameters like end-of-speech timeouts, and customized vocabularies.

Barge-In

Another aspect of speech recognition technology that heavily affects your design is the use of barge-in. That is, will you allow your users to interrupt the system when it's talking?

Barge-in is generally turned on for interactive voice response (IVR) systems, so the user can interrupt the system at any time. When the system detects speech of any kind, it immediately stops playing the current prompt and begins listening, as demonstrated in the following example:

> **BANKING IVR**
> You can transfer money, check your account balance, pay a...
>
> **USER**
> *[interrupting]* Check my account balance.

In the IVR world, barge-in makes a lot of sense. There are often long menus or lists of options, and it's tedious to always force users to wait. This is especially true for IVR systems that users call regularly.

When you allow barge-in, you must be extra careful with pauses in the prompt as well as placement of questions. Here are some examples of where things can go wrong:

> **VUI SYSTEM**
> What would you like to do? *[1-second silence]* You...
>
> **USER**
> I would...
>
> **VUI SYSTEM**
> *[system continues]* can. *[then stops because user has barged in]*
>
> **USER**
> *[stops]*

In the previous example, the system paused briefly after the initial question. At that point, the user began to speak, but just at that moment, the system continued with its next instruction. Now the user thinks they've interrupted the system before it was finished and stops talking, but it's too late: the system has stopped talking, as well. The conversation has been broken, and it will take an error prompt to get the user back on track. Imagine talking to someone on a bad cell phone connection—there can be a noticeable lag that doesn't exist in person, and callers often talk over each other.

The example has a second problem. When the system asked the user a question, the user naturally responded. Avoid asking a question and following it with more information, because users tend to respond to the question and will begin speaking before the prompt is finished. It's best to list what you can do, followed by the question:

VUI SYSTEM
You can check your balance, transfer funds, or speak to an agent. What would you like to do?

Barge-in is also very useful when the system is performing an action that can take a long time or reciting a lot of information. For example, when the Amazon Echo is playing a song, you can barge in at any time and say, "Alexa, stop." Without barge-in, there would be no way to stop playing music by using a voice command.

Unlike traditional IVR systems, however, Alexa does not stop speaking when just *any* speech is detected—only her wake word does that. This is sometimes referred to as a *hotword* or *magic word*. It's a very neat trick because it does not stop the system from performing/speaking unless a particular keyword or phrase has been recognized. This is very important in certain situations. Imagine you've asked Alexa to play a particular Pandora radio station. Meanwhile, you begin chatting with your family. Having Alexa say, "Sorry, what was that?" after you spoke would be a terrible user experience. Instead, she happily ignores you until her wake word has been confidently recognized.

Hotwords are used in the IVR world as well, but in specific contexts. One example is the San Francisco Bay Area 511 IVR system (for which I was the lead VUI designer). Users can call to get traffic information and estimated driving times, among other things. After giving the name of a highway, the system looks for relevant traffic incidents and begins reading them back to the caller. I wanted to allow users the flexibility of skipping ahead to the next incident, but worried about background noise in the car or other input interrupting the system and stopping it. Imagine that you're listening to a list of 10 traffic incidents, and you sneeze and the system stops and says, "I'm sorry, I didn't get that." You would need to start all over!

Instead, using the hotword technique, only a few key phrases are recognized during this readback, such as "next" and "previous." When the user speaks, the system does not immediately cut off the prompt, as is done in normal barge-in mode, but continues unless one of the keywords was recognized, only then stopping and moving on to the next action.

Another example for which using a hotword is useful is when the user needs to pause to complete an action in the middle of a conversation. This could occur if a user needs to go and grab something to answer a question, such as getting a pill bottle to check a prescription number in the middle of requesting a refill. The system asks, "Do you need some time to find the prescription number?" and if the user says "yes," the system instructs the user to say "I'm back" or "continue" when they're ready, essentially putting the conversation on pause.

For VUI systems that are not voice-only, barge-in is not always advised. When using prerecorded video, for example, barge-in should not be used, because it is difficult to know what to do with video in that case. Would the video of the actor suddenly stop? Would it then shift to a prerecorded video of the actor having been interrupted?

When your VUI system has an avatar or prerecorded video, it's much more similar to a real human conversation, and users tend to be more polite and wait the system out. They also engage in side speech (talking to someone else) while the avatar or video is speaking, clearly showing they don't expect the avatar to be listening at that point.

If your system does not have barge-in enabled, do not force the user to listen to long lists or long menus. Instead, break things into more steps and rely on visual lists to reduce cognitive load. For example, if the user must choose from a list of seven video clip titles, it's not a good idea to say them all out loud. Instead, you can use visually displayed information, as demonstrated here and in Figure 4-1:

USER
Show me the funniest clips with orangutans.

Here are some matching videos.

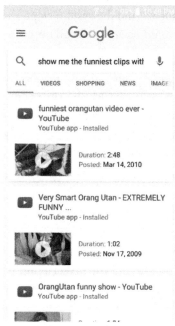

FIGURE 4-1.

Google displays a list of videos instead of saying them out loud

Imagine having the phone read out all those titles. Unless there is a reason the user cannot look at the screen (such as being visually impaired), it's much smoother to display them graphically.

As a final note on barge-in, it is possible to fine-tune its sensitivity with some ASR tools. Essentially, you can make it more or less sensitive (the less sensitive it is, the more difficult it is for users to barge in).

Timeouts

In addition to paying attention to when the user is speaking, it's important for a VUI system to know when the user *stops* speaking. Being able to detect when someone has finished their question or response is essential to a good VUI experience. Without this, the user is not sure whether the system heard them. In addition to losing faith in the system, the conversation becomes more difficult as the user and the system engage in an awkward dance of starting and stopping to speak. Have you ever been on a video chat in which there is a slight lag? It seems so minor, but when you don't know when the other person has finished speaking, authentic conversation is difficult and painful.

End-of-speech timeout

As mentioned earlier, one of the most important things for a good VUI experience is good endpoint detection, which means, knowing when the user has finished talking (in other words, finished their turn in the conversation).

Some speech recognition engines allow you to configure endpoint detection by setting what is sometimes referred to as the *end-of-speech timeout*. This refers to the length of the pause in what the user is saying before the system decides that the user is finished speaking.

Not all speech recognition engines allow you to set the end-of-speech timeout, but it is useful to know what their defaults are. A pause of 1.5 seconds is a good rule of thumb for most types of VUI responses. Make it too short and you'll cut off the user before they've finished speaking; make it too long and the user will wonder if the system heard them.

There are instances for which you will want to adjust this timeout if you're able. The most well-designed VUI systems are flexible enough to have different timeout values at different states. For example, a user-initiated interaction (such as saying, "Ok Google," or pressing the Apple home button to activate Siri) needs a shorter timeout than the response to "How are you doing today?" In the first case, because the *user* initiated the event and not the system, it is likely that the user knows exactly what they're going to say and will not need a long pause. In the second case, the user might stop and start a bit; for example, "I'm feeling...well, earlier I was OK, but now I...my head is hurting." In this case, if the timeout is too short, the user will be cut off before they've finished, which is very rude in conversations.

Another common case for which a longer end-of-speech timeout is needed is when people read a number that's naturally grouped, such as a credit card. People naturally pause between groups, and you don't want to cut them off.

The best way to know how to adjust it is to use data. By looking at transcriptions of what people actually said, you can find places in which users are often cut off mid-sentence. In this case, you will want to experiment with extending the end-of-speech timeout.

One area where extending the length of the timeout is helpful is when you expect the user to speak a lot or to hesitate. For example, asking the user to recount the details of a car accident for an insurance app. The user will likely say multiple sentences, pausing occasionally while gathering their thoughts.

In certain cases, it's also a good idea to *shorten* the end-of-speech timeout. When users are merely saying "yes" or "no," a shorter timeout can lead to a snappier, more responsive dialog.

No speech timeout

Another important timeout is for no speech detected (NSP). This should be treated as a separate timeout from end-of-speech for several reasons:

- The NSP timeout is longer than the end-of-speech timeout (usually around 10 seconds).

- NSP timeouts result in different actions by the VUI system.

- It's helpful for system analysis to determine where there are problems.

In IVR systems, an NSP timeout occurs when the recognizer begins listening for a user response and does not detect any speech for a certain length of time. It's then up to the VUI designer to decide what to do in this case. With IVR systems, the user is commonly given an error message, such as, "Sorry, I didn't hear that. What day are you traveling?" and waits for the user to speak.

Some systems do nothing when the NSP timeout is triggered. For example, if you say, "Alexa," to activate the Amazon Echo and then don't say anything else, after about eight seconds the blue light at the top of the device will turn off and Alexa will remain silent.

Ok Google (Figure 4-2) waits about five seconds, and if nothing is said, it pops up a screen with examples of what you can say, such as "Call Pizza Hut" and "Show me pictures of cats" (the most common use of the Internet). Siri and Cortana also provide examples after a timeout (Figures 4-3 and 4-4).

Say "Ok Google" or tap mic

Movies nearby

Call Pizza Hut

What's the weather?

Turn up the volume

Call Sophie

Show me pictures of cats

Set a timer for 10 minutes

Show me puppy videos

Show my agenda

FIGURE 4-2.
Ok Google's response to NSP: it lists things you can say

Some things you can ask me:

Wake me up in 8 hours

Get a table for three tonight

Find my meeting notes

Call Brian

Enable Wi-Fi

FIGURE 4-3.
Siri's NSP: it also lists things you can say

FIGURE 4-4.
Cortana's NSP: she greets you by name and suggests things that you can say

As mentioned in Chapter 2, doing nothing is sometimes a fine design choice. In these cases, it's clear to users that they were not heard, and they'll generally try again.

These examples—wherein the system does not explicitly prompt the user on an NSP timeout—illustrate the different modes of VUIs that are common today. Many of these virtual assistants are still in "one-off" mode: they expect the user to say something, and respond to it, and generally the conversation is over, until the user initiates a new request. In the IVR world, the user is in the middle of a dialog, and would not be able to advance without getting more input, so prompting the user on an NSP timeout makes more sense.

Another case (as mentioned in Chapters 2 and 3) for which doing nothing is fine is when you have a video or avatar. If the system doesn't hear you, it continues to *look* expectantly, which is a common cue in human conversation that the person you're speaking to did not hear you.

Is it important, however, to do more for the NSP event when the user is stuck. If you're in a conversational system with an avatar and multiple NSP timeouts have been triggered, give the user a way out. If the system already has a graphical user interface (GUI) displayed (such as buttons on the screen), that is sufficient. GUIs can wait until the user performs an action—think about a website; there is no timeout there (unless you're buying concert tickets).

But in a voice-only system, employ "just in time" help. One example comes from a Volio-created iPad app that uses prerecorded video (*http:// bit.ly/2hcpvv4/*). The app simulates a conversation with one of *Esquire* magazine's columnists, Rodney Cutler, giving advice about hair products. During the conversation, the user's face is shown in the picture-in-picture window in the upper-right corner. When it's time for the user to speak, the box around their face lights up in green (Figure 4-5).

If no speech is detected, nothing happens—the actor continues to engage in "active listening," nodding occasionally and looking at the user.

If multiple NSP timeouts have been detected in the first state, the app throws up a caption: "Say something—it's your turn to speak!"

In another one of the *Esquire* conversations, users speak with columnist Nick Sullivan about what to wear on a date. This example shows what happens later on in the app, after multiple misrecognitions or NSP timeouts. First, the icon in the upper-right corner flashes gently. When the user taps it, a drop-down list of possible options appears, letting the user use touch to proceed (Figure 4-6). It then disappears.

FIGURE 4-5.
Example of "just in time" help after several NSP timeouts; the user is visually prompted

FIGURE 4-6.
After numerous NSP timeouts, a drop-down list of choices is provided

While designing your system, spend some time thinking about *why* the NSP timeout might have been triggered. First, although the system *thinks* it did not hear any speech, it could be mistaken. It's possible a user did speak, but it was not picked up by the recognizer.

Some designers create prompts that say things like "Speak louder" or "Get closer to the microphone." But these can be very frustrating: if the user spoke too softly to be heard, telling them to speak louder only encourages them to over-articulate individual words, and this rarely solves the recognition problem. Instead, design around how to get the user to the next step. Often, this means letting users repeat themselves, or after multiple NSP timeouts, providing an alternative way to give input.

There are times, of course, when the user really did not say anything. Again, with your designer hat on, consider why this might be. If your data shows there is a particular place in your app in which users don't speak, examine the interaction more closely. Here's an example of an app that allows users to pay their Internet service provider (ISP) bills, with a question that leads to frequent NSP timeouts. The following example shows how to handle it poorly:

ISP VUI
What's your account number?

USER
[silence]

ISP VUI
I'm sorry, I didn't hear anything. Please say your account number.

USER
[silence]

ISP VUI
I still didn't hear anything. Please say your account number.

As you can imagine, this does not lead to a successful outcome. The reason is because the user is given no help. The system simply repeats the question.

Why do you think this particular question led to a lot of NSP timeouts? Imagine the user is trying to pay their balance, but they don't know their account number. What can they do? Here's an example that lets them keep going:

ISP VUI
What's your account number?

USER
[silence]

ISP VUI
Sorry, I didn't get that. Your account number can be found at the top of your statement. Please say or type it in, or say, "I don't know it."

USER
I don't know it.

ISP VUI
No problem. We can look it up with your phone number and address instead...

What was better about this example? First, it lets the user know where they can find their account number, if they have their statement. Second, it lets the user continue another way, if they don't know or can't find their account number.

Too much speech

Another timeout (used less frequently) is *too-much-speech* (TMS). This is triggered in the case of a user talking for a very long time, with no pauses that would have normally triggered the end-of-speech timeout. For most systems, it's not generally necessary to handle this instance, because the user will need to take a breath at some point. It's a good idea to still be on the lookout for these events in deployed applications because it might indicate that the recognizer is triggering on nonsalient speech, and you need to determine why.

However, if you find yourself designing a system that encourages users to speak for lengthy segments, and the length of utterances goes on too long, you can institute a TMS timeout and cut off the user in order to move on in the conversation. It's best to look at data to determine your TMS timeout, but you can begin with something that's not too short (and would cut users off too easily), such as 7 to 10 seconds.

N-Best Lists

Moving on from types of timeouts, let's look more closely at what the system returns when it *does* recognize something.

A recognition engine does not typically return just one result for what it thinks the user said. Instead, it returns what's referred to as an *N*-best list, which is a list of what the user might have said, ordered by likelihood (usually the top 5 or 10 possibilities), as well as the confidence score. Suppose that you're designing a fun VUI app that lets people talk about their favorite animal:

MY FAVORITE ANIMAL VUI
So, I really want to know more about what animals you love. What's your favorite?

USER
Well, I think at the moment my favorite's gotta be...kitty cats!

OK, let's take a peek behind the scenes now. At this point, the ASR tool will be returning a list of what it actually recognized, and the app must decide what to do next. Let's look at the N-best list, which begins with the utterance about which it is the most confident. Note that speech recognition engines do not always return capitalization or punctuation:

1. WELL I THINK AT THE MOMENT MY FAVORITES GOT TO BE FIT AND FAT

2. WELL I THINK AT THE MOMENT BY FAVORITES GOTTA BE KITTY CATS

3. WELL I HAVE AT THE MOMENT MY FAN IS OF THE KITTY

4. WELL I HAVE AT THE MOMENT MY FAN IS OF THE KITTY BAT

5. WELL THAT THE MOMENT MY FAVORITE IS GOT TO BE KIT AND CAT

You've designed your system to look for animal names, and have an entire list of valid examples, including "cat," "dog," "horse," "penguin," "caracal," and so on. If your VUI looked only at the first item in the N-best list, it would fail to make a match, and return a "no match" to the system, leading to prompt the user with something such as, "I'm sorry, I didn't get that...what's your favorite animal?"

Instead, what if we take advantage of our N-best list? When the first one results in no match, move on to the next—and there we find "cat." Success!

Another way the N-best list is useful is when users are correcting information. Without the N-best list, you might continue suggesting the same incorrect option, over and over:

TRAVEL VUI
What city are you starting from?

USER
Boston.

TRAVEL VUI
Was that Austin?

USER
No, Boston.

TRAVEL VUI
Was that Austin?

USER
No, Boston!

TRAVEL VUI
....Austin?

As you might imagine, that becomes annoying fast. If your VUI takes advantage of the *N*-Best list, however, you can put rejects on a skip list; thus, if Austin is the number one item the next time, move to the next one on the list.

The Challenges of Speech Recognition

We've talked about the ways you can harness the best features of speech recognition engines. Now, we need to talk about the places where the technology is not quite there yet.

Although some statistics show ASR has greater than 90 percent accuracy, keep in mind this is under ideal conditions. Ideal conditions typically mean an adult male in a quiet room with a good microphone.

Then we have the real world...

This section covers some of the challenges you'll face that are unique to designing VUIs. Many of these are, as a VUI designer, out of your control. Besides waiting for the technology to improve, your job is to know these things exist and do your best to design around them.

Noise

One of the most difficult challenges for ASR tools is handling noise. This includes constant noise, such as that heard while driving on the freeway, or sitting in a busy restaurant or near a water fountain. It can also include noise that occurred just when the user spoke, such as the bark of a dog or vegetables hitting a hot frying pan while cooking in the kitchen.

Other challenges include side speech (when the user talks to a friend or coworker as an aside, while the app is listening), a television on in the background, or multiple people speaking at the same time.

As I mentioned just a moment ago, there is not a lot you can do about these challenges as the VUI designer, so the best thing to do is remember your user will have times when, for whatever reason, the system did not understand her—all you can do is follow the techniques described in this book to help alleviate this as much as possible. Occasionally apps try to guess what the issue is and instruct the user to move to a less noisy environment, get closer to the mic, and so on, but there is too much danger in guessing wrong and annoying your user with these suggestions. Instead, focus on providing help via escalating error behavior and offering other ways than voice for the user to continue.

The technology continues to improve remarkably. I have been in crowded, noisy restaurants with a band playing, and the ASR in my phone app still managed to understand a search query. Improved microphone direction on mobile phones is getting better, as well, which helps a lot.

Multiple Speakers

A poster named danieltobey on the website Reddit explained why he disabled allowing his phone to be woken up by saying "Ok Google":

> I work in a small office with a few other people, each of whom own Android smartphones. One day we realized that all of us had the "Ok Google" phrase enabled on our phones. Every time any of us said "OK Google" louder than a whisper (quiet office), all of our phones would wake up and start listening.
>
> Needless to say, shortly thereafter all of us disabled this feature on our phones. Although it was nice to be able to say, "Ok Google, remind me to bring my lunchbag home later today," it wasn't as nice to have everyone else be reminded to bring my lunchbag home, as well.

Although new technology is evolving that will allow users to train their device to only respond to their own voice (as of this writing, Google has a primitive version of this running), discerning who is speaking is still a challenge for VUIs. If the user is in the middle of a query ("Hey, Siri, can you please tell me the top-rated restaurants in Walnut Creek, California") and your coworker starts talking, how does the computer know who to listen to?

Additionally, as Karen Kaushansky pointed out in her 2016 talk at the O'Reilly Design Conference, there is a corollary issue: which device should respond when I make a request? Imagine you have an Apple Watch, an iPhone, and your car responds to voice commands, too. If you're driving and you say, "Tell me the score of last night's game," which device (or vehicle) should respond (Figure 4-7)?

FIGURE 4-7.
Which should respond to voice: your watch or your phone or your car? (Photo used with permission from K. Kaushansky)

The answer is simple: whichever one is appropriate. I cover this topic in more detail in Chapter 8.

Children

At this time, children (especially very young children) are much more difficult for ASR tools to recognize accurately. Part of that is because children have shorter vocal tracts, and thus higher pitched-voices, and there is much less data for that type of speech (although that is changing). Another reason is because young children are more likely to meander, stutter, have long pauses, and repeat themselves.

If you're designing an app specifically for kids, keep this in mind. Two common design practices are useful here:

- When designing games or other conversational apps, allow interactions in which it's not vital to understand 100 percent perfectly to move on. For example, Mattel and ToyTalk's Hello Barbie (Figure 4-8) asks "What would you like to be when you grow up?" In addition to having responses for things it recognizes confidently, such as "veterinarian" and "CEO of a tech startup," it could have a general response for when there is a no match, such as having Barbie say, "Sounds good. I want to be a space horticulturalist!" The conversation moves naturally along, even if a specific response was not provided.

- For cases in which the information is needed, offer graphical alternatives. For example, a pain management app might ask kids where it hurts; offer a graphic of the human body for kids to identify where the pain is felt as well.

These strategies apply to adults for users of all ages but can be particularly helpful for kids.

FIGURE 4-8.
Hello Barbie from Mattel and ToyTalk (*http://hellobarbiefaq.mattel.com/*)

Names, Spelling, and Alphanumeric

Some specific types of responses are more difficult for ASR tools than others. Very short phrases such as "yes" and "no" are much more difficult to recognize than longer ones, such as "Yes, I will" and "No, thank you." Shorter utterances simply have less data for the tool to process. Encouraging your user to speak naturally rather than robotically can often result in *higher* recognition accuracy.

Nowadays, another reason is that the more context the ASR tool has, the better. ASR tools have learned a great deal about language and what people actually say, and they use this information to improve their models. As you speak, the tool is modifying its recognition result, as demonstrated in Figure 4-9.

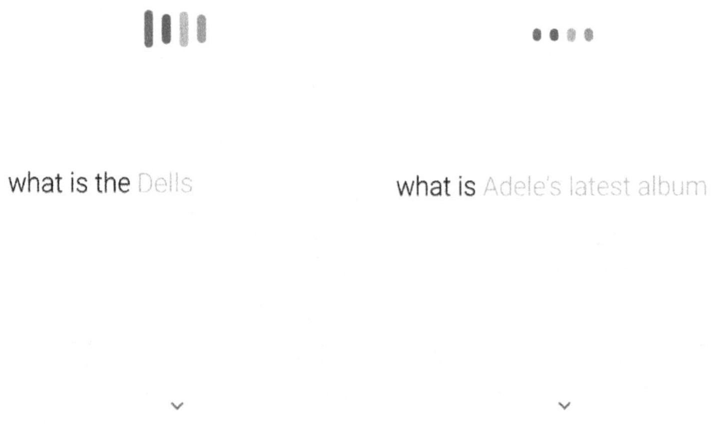

ll￭l￭   **● ● ● ●**

what is the Dells   what is Adele's latest album

⌄   ⌄

FIGURE 4-9.
As I say "What is Adele's latest album," the recognition result for Ok Google dynamically changes from "What is the Dells" to "what is Adele's latest album"

Names, spelling, and alphanumeric strings are also tough. This is when having a GUI can be extremely valuable, because you can ask users to type these sorts of items, ensuring better accuracy. Names are tricky because there is such an enormous variety and many ways to spell the same name. Take "Cathy," for example. If I say my name and the system recognized "Kathy," and then tries to look up my reservation, it will fail. Even people have difficulty understanding names spelled one letter at a time; hence, the need for the "phonetic alphabet" that we often hear used by military and law enforcement personnel—alpha, bravo, Charlie, and so on.

If your user chooses to say those items—or if you have no GUI option available—your best bet is to take advantage of known data. Some examples of this include the following:

- Credit card checksums (an algorithm to determine if a sequence of numbers is a valid credit card number)
- List of registered user names
- Postal code verification (e.g., in the United Kingdom, determining if a given postal code, such as NG9 5BL, follows a valid postcode format)
- Cities closest to the current known location

By using these prepopulated lists and contexts, you can throw out the invalid results at runtime, and prioritize which ones are more likely.

Data Privacy

When users are finally trying out your app and you begin to collect data, it's a very exciting time. You'll be eager to see what people say to your system, and to use that information to improve it. But ensure that you have basic privacy checks in place. You might have the best of intentions, but that doesn't make it OK.

Don't store data that wasn't meant for you. If you have a device that is constantly listening for a wake word, do not keep what the user says that doesn't come before the wake word. Users expect and deserve privacy, and this data should not be preserved or stored, even anonymously. Given that more and more speech-activated devices are being used in homes, it's important to put standards in place that prioritize privacy, and will reassure users.

The Amazon Echo is always listening for its wake word "Alexa," but this speech recognition is performed locally, on the device. The audio is thrown away unless and until "Alexa" has been recognized, at which point the cloud-based recognition takes over. The Jibo family robot follows the same approach. It's always listening, but until you say, "Hey, Jibo," it won't store your speech.

Mattel and ToyTalk's interactive Hello Barbie only listens when her belt buckle is pushed on (push-to-talk), so it does not listen in on all the conversations the child might be having.

For data that does apply to your system—that is, the user is talking to your app/device—make sure it is stripped of all information that could tie it to the user. You can keep audio samples, but do not associate those with account numbers, birthdays, and so on. You should also consider stripping sensitive information from recognition results in application logs.

Conclusion

As a VUI designer, it's important to understand the underpinnings of the technology for which you're designing. Knowing the strengths and weaknesses of ASR tools can put your app ahead of the others in terms of performance. Having a system with good recognition accuracy is only part of the story; the design around what's recognized plays a crucial part in a good user experience.

Understanding barge-in, timeouts, endpoint detection, and the challenges of different environments will help you to create the best VUI possible.

[5]

Advanced Voice User Interface Design

In Chapter 2, we went over voice user interface (VUI) design basics. In this chapter, we cover topics related to making your VUI not merely functional and usable, but beyond. Here, we take a look at what will make it most engaging, easy to use, and successful.

Siri and the Amazon Echo are both examples of popular VUIs. The Echo has recently received a lot of praise about its interface. Given that the two systems can do many similar things, why is the Echo often a better user experience? One reason is that the Echo was designed with voice in mind from the beginning—that's its sole purpose. Siri, by comparison, is just one more way to interact with your iPhone.

As Kathryn Whitenton writes: "The Echo, on the other hand, prioritizes voice interaction above all else." She goes on:

> Siri's ability to expedite web searches with voice input for queries is certainly valuable, but the bias toward interpreting user questions as web searches can actually increase error rates when doing other tasks. The benefit of the Echo's more focused functionality is even more apparent if you need multiple timers (not an uncommon scenario when cooking). When asked to set a new timer, Alexa easily responds, "Second timer set for 40 minutes, starting now," while Siri, which only has one timer, balks: "Your timer's already running, at 9 minutes and 42 seconds. Would you like to change it?
>
> But for short tasks, failing to hear a command the first time can easily tip the balance, and make the voice system more cumbersome and time consuming than an existing physical alternative, such as glancing at a digital timer or walking across the room to flip a light switch. New

technologies must make tasks faster and easier in order to be viable replacements for existing tools. For short tasks, voice detection errors can make this impossible.[1]

Much of what has been discussed so far relates to the speech recognition piece of VUIs, and not the natural-language understanding (NLU) part. Speech recognition refers to the words that the recognition engine returns; NLU is how you interpret those responses. Today, with the improvements in speech recognition accuracy, the challenges of designing a good VUI lie more in the NLU—the way the input is handled—than in the technology itself.

Let's begin by looking at the various ways a VUI can respond to input.

Branching Based on Voice Input

To this point in the book, we have not spent a lot of time discussing how to handle different types of valid voice input. Not all input will be the same: what we expect the user to say, and how to handle it, can vary from turn to turn.

We'll begin with the more basic types of responses, and move on from there.

Constrained Responses

Sometimes, the system is asking a very basic question, such as, "Did you want me to book the flight?" or "What's your favorite color?" These types of questions have a very constrained set of responses. For the first case, we just need to look for variations on "yes" and "no." In the second case, we will have a list of accepted colors. If the user says something outside this narrow domain, it will not be handled.

Here are some examples of constrained responses:

- Yes: yes, yeah, sure, of course, yep

- No: nope, naw, nah, no

- Colors: red, yellow, blue, green, purple, magenta, pink, white, black, chartreuse, maroon, gray

---

1 Whitenton, K. (2016). "The Most Important Design Principles Of Voice UX." Retrieved from *https://www.fastcodesign.com/*.

When the recognition result is returned by the automated speech recognition (ASR tool), we have a straightforward search task: does one of the items from the expected list appear in the recognition result? For example, if the user says, "Yes, I would very much like you to book my flight," we have found the word "yes" and we have a match. The task is complete.

Here are some other examples that include constrained responses:

- "Please tell me the name of the restaurant you're looking for"
- "What city are you traveling to?"
- "What is your main symptom?"
- "What song would you like to hear?"

In some of these, the lists themselves could be quite lengthy, but it's still a constrained category that will have only one result.

When mapping multiple ways to say the same thing into one bucket, be aware of what the follow-up prompt sounds like. In one chatbot example I saw, the bot asked the question, "Do you understand what that means?" and allowed for three possible responses: "That's deep," "Not really," and "Lame." It mapped my typed response, "yes," to "that's deep." This made perfect sense from a flow standpoint—it did have the same meaning, essentially—but the next prompt was, "I fail to see what depth has to do with it," which felt like a strange response for "yes."

It's also important to map common incorrect recognition results to the right place. For example, the word "fine," on its own, is often misrecognized as "find." I've seen this occur frequently as a response to the question "How are you?"

[NOTE]

Short words are often more difficult to interpret and handle in terms of speech recognition than longer phrases, so "I am fine" is more likely to be recognized correctly than just "fine."

To solve this, it's possible to map the word "find" to "fine" in these states. Another example is a user who asked, "What is the pool depth?" but the recognizer returned "what is the pool death." If this is a common occurrence, adding "pool death" to the accepted key phrases is straightforward. In addition, using an *N*-best list would help with this issue; "pool depth" is a likely occurrence later in the list, and walking through it until a more relevant match occurs, rather than just choosing the first, will automatically improve your VUI's accuracy.

Open Speech

Another technique that can be especially useful in conversational VUI apps (not just one-offs) is a technique that we (myself, Mark Anikst, and Lisa Falkson) developed at Volio to handle cases in which we wanted the conversation to flow naturally, but did not necessarily need to explicitly handle the input.

For example, in the Volio app with a stand-up comic, the dialog (written by Robbie Pickard) was as follows:

> COMEDIAN
> Man, you're up early. I'm a comedian; I usually sleep 'til noon. What are you doing up?
>
> USER
> I got up early to have a big breakfast!
>
> COMEDIAN
> Lucky you. I woke up to the vacuum blasting at 6 AM.

Here's the same app, but the user responds differently:

> COMEDIAN
> Man, you're up early. I'm a comedian; I usually sleep 'til noon. What are you doing up?
>
> USER
> Man...I gotta go to work.
>
> COMEDIAN
> Lucky you. I woke up to the vacuum blasting at 6 AM.

In this case, the response the user gave was not critical to the next piece of the conversation, so giving a general reply was appropriate.

Another strategy is to let the user know someone else (such as a doctor) will be listening to their answers later, as shown in this health app example:

VIRTUAL NURSE
Please tell me a little more about the headaches you've been having.

USER
Well, they usually start in the evening and last a couple of hours.

VIRTUAL NURSE
Thank you. I will share this with your doctor.

This is a great way to obtain information in a natural, conversational mode, even if the VUI doesn't handle it explicitly. In these instances, it's important that the user is made fully aware of who will review this information so there will not be a violation of trust.

Categorization of Input

Sometimes, rather than have a specific set of items in a category, you might want to do a broader categorization, such as "good" and "bad," or "happy mood" and "sad mood." In these cases, the set of responses to look for simply map to a category rather than an exact item.

How are you feeling?

- Happy: happy, joyful, great, excited, good
- Sad: sad, depressed, bad, unhappy, miserable

The VUI can then handle these, not as specific items, but as *categories*.

VIRTUAL COMPANION
How are you feeling?

USER
Well...kind of depressed, to be honest.

VIRTUAL COMPANION
I'm sorry to hear that. Want to tell me more?

Notice the virtual companion did not say, "It sounds like you're depressed." In this case, there is no need to confirm the exact way the user expressed their low mood—just to acknowledge it in general.

Wildcards and Logical Expressions

Looking for specific keywords, or key phrases, can go a long way, but to level up to the next step in NLU, it's useful to allow for more complex specifications. A *wildcard* allows for more flexibility by allowing certain words to be repeated without having to specify them explicitly.

A wildcard scenario can be helpful, so the same word could be repeated:

- My computer is really* slow ("My computer is slow." "My computer is really slow." "My computer is really really slow.")

Logical expressions will also open up your recognition accuracy. Imagine that you're building a technical support VUI to help people with computer problems. You might begin with a straightforward list of key phrases, such as the following:

- Blue screen of death

- Internet is not working

- Forgot my password

- Printer won't print

You will quickly realize that the way people phrase these problems can be quite varied, and writing every variation is an enormous task. However, there are common patterns. Add the ability for and/or, and you can have things like this:

- Forgot AND password ("My dad forgot his password again," "I don't remember my password...I forgot it.")

All of these add a great deal to your recognition accuracy without a huge amount of overhead.

Disambiguation

This leads us to the next area of complexity: disambiguation.

Humans are not always clear. Even when we talk to other humans, we often need to ask follow-up questions to ensure that we understand what the other person meant. Imagine you work at a café, and a customer walks up and says, "I'd like a large, please." You might be pretty sure they're talking about ordering a coffee, but because you have other items, as well, you need to ask a follow-up question: "Did you want a large coffee, tea, or juice?"

VUIs will of course encounter the same situations.

Not Enough Information

As demonstrated in the preceding example of a customer simply ordering a "large," people do not always give enough information to complete the task. Take the example of asking for the weather in Springfield. In the United States, there are 34 towns and cities named Springfield. If I am in the United States and I say, "What's the weather in Springfield?", the system should ask me which state. When thinking about this example, I decided to try a few different virtual assistants and see how they handled it. I was rather surprised to discover that *none* of them disambiguated. All seven that I tried just chose the city for me, without any follow-up! (All of them did correctly recognize "What's the weather in Springfield?" because I could see the result displayed on the screen.) I'm in California, but the cities that the virtual assistants selected ranged dramatically, as Table 5-1 clearly shows. One, in fact, never told me the state, but simply said "Springfield," so I still have no idea which one it chose (Figure 5-1).

TABLE 5-1. The range of "Springfields" selected by seven virtual assistants

VIRTUAL ASSISTANT	SPRINGFIELD
Hound	Springfield, Oregon
Cortana	Springfield, Illinois
Api.ai Assistant	Springfield, Illinois
Siri	Springfield, Missouri
Google	Springfield, Missouri
Alexa	Central Coast, Australia
Robin	Springfield, ???

FIGURE 5-1.

I'm not even sure which
Springfield Robin chose

Let's design an example of a better way to handle this case:

USER
What's the weather in Springfield?

VIRTUAL ASSISTANT
Springfield...in which state?

USER
Illinois, please.

VIRTUAL ASSISTANT
In Springfield, Illinois, it's currently 75 degrees.

Another example that falls into the "not enough information" category is missing intent. In the tech support example, if a user says, "I need help with the Internet," perhaps they mean their Internet connection isn't working or that they need help setting up WiFi. Rather than dismiss their query entirely because there is no exact match, keep a list of common topics, and follow up by asking for intent:

TECH SUPPORT ASSISTANT
Hi there, I'm Pat, your tech support assistant. How can I help you today?

USER

I need help with the Internet.

TECH SUPPORT ASSISTANT

Internet. Sure, I can help with that. Let me get some more information from you first.

I can help you set up your WiFi, find information online, or fix your Internet connection. Which one do you need help with?

More Than One Piece of Information When Only One Is Expected

Another situation in which disambiguation is needed is when the user gives *too* much information. This often occurs when the user is asked for one specific item but, naturally, provides more. For example, a medical app might ask, "What is your main symptom?" It's possible it's only programmed to handle one symptom at a time—but people will often say more, such as, "I have a fever and a cough."

There are several strategies at this point:

- Take the first symptom recognized (fever)
- Reject the entire response because "fever and a cough" is not one of the available symptoms
- Disambiguate

The ideal technique is to disambiguate. You don't need to hide the fact that you need to do one symptom at a time—let the user help:

HEALTH ASSISTANT

What is your main symptom?

USER

I have a fever and a cough.

HEALTH ASSISTANT

Which one of those would you say is bothering you the most right now?

USER

The cough...it's pretty bad.

HEALTH ASSISTANT

OK, let's start with the cough. I can also help with the fever symptom later.

In this case, the system has simply asked the user to focus first on the most pressing symptom. This can still be a helpful, useful experience. Two other notes on this design:

- If the user said up front they had a fever, don't ask about it later when asking questions about their cough. The system will lose credibility.

- Creators of VUI systems often think that if they just put all the instructions up front, people will say the right thing. You might be tempted to change the initial prompt to "Please tell me your main symptom, but only one." This is not advisable. First, it makes the dialog less natural. Second, a lot of users will ignore it anyway. You still need to build in a way to respond. Doing user testing (with real users out in the world) will also help you to craft prompts to elicit the best responses.

A different example of this is when users say "both," as in the following example:

VIRTUAL ASSISTANT
Which one would you like, a map or the phone number?

USER
Both.

VIRTUAL ASSISTANT
OK, I'll give you a map first and then the phone number.

A common example where disambiguation is used is for making phone calls. If I ask Google to call someone in my Contacts list, and there is more than one phone number listed, it shows both and asks me to disambiguate by saying, "Sure. Mobile or work?"

If I say nothing, Google adds additional help by saying, "To keep going, just say which phone number you want to use. For instance, you can say 'the first one.'" It's multimodal, of course: I can also tap the one I want (Figure 5-2). Being able to use my voice is important here because I might be driving or otherwise need hands-free interaction.

This is a common workflow. Api's Assistant uses a similar method, as depicted in Figure 5-3.

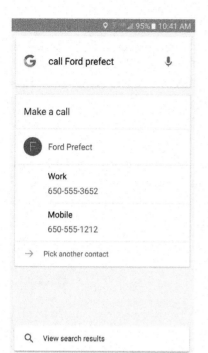

FIGURE 5-2.
Google disambiguating:
which number do you
want to call?

FIGURE 5-3.
Assistant's call
disambiguation

I have noticed improvements to these systems over time. In the past, when I asked to text a contact, for example, Google asked if I wanted to text the home or mobile number. Recently, it defaults to the mobile number, which makes sense given that it's impossible to text someone's home phone.

Handling Negation

Recently I tried out a pizza chatbot. It asked me for toppings, and I typed "Mushrooms, but no pepperoni!" The confirmation (see Figure 5-4) displayed, "OK, I have one Large Mushrooms & Pepperoni pizza for delivery. Is that correct?"

FIGURE 5-4.
Pizza chatbot ignores
the negative

This illustrates the importance of looking out for negative responses, such as "not," "no," and "neither." Imagine how the dialog would sound if upon asking, "How are you feeling today?" the user says "Not very good," and your VUI (matching on the word "good") responds with a cheery "Great to hear!" Your user will probably think your VUI is either sarcastic or stupid, neither of which makes a great impression. Handling these takes more work, but the cost of ignoring them can be high.

Hound has a good example of handling this well: when I say, "Show me nearby Asian restaurants except for Japanese," it manages to do just that (Figure 5-5).

FIGURE 5-5.

Hound handling exceptions in a restaurant search

Capturing Intent and Objects

As your VUI becomes more complex, your strategies for handling speech input must become smarter. The previous examples generally have one "intent," or action, that the user wants to take. In the disambiguation example, when the user said "Internet," the system asked a clarifying question to determine *what* the user needed help with in terms of their Internet connection.

More advanced systems can determine the intent upon an object on its own. For example, with a virtual assistant such as Siri, there are multiple things you can do with the calendar: view your calendar, add events, and cancel events. In this type of system, simply matching on the keyword "calendar" will not be good enough. Instead, your VUI's NLU model must be trained to understand that the following sentences, although all related to the calendar, will ultimately result in different actions:

- Show me my calendar

- Add an event to my calendar

- Delete my meeting from my calendar

Building these types of models (and more complex ones) is beyond the scope of this book. There are third-party tools that you can use to create these more complex models. These tools provide sample sets of examples that allow you to build up a more complex set of ways in which users can interact with your VUI. Some examples of tools include Api.ai (now owned by Google), Nuance Mix, Wit.ai (Facebook), Houndify, Microsoft LUIS, and Amazon Echo.

Dialog Management

To make your VUI as flexible as possible, a concept called *dialog management* will become important. Dialog management is how the system manages what has already occurred in the conversation, and what needs to happen next. This is important because users want to provide information in different ways; someone will give all the information up front, and some will provide it piece by piece. To handle this, the app needs to know what bits of information are needed (these bits are sometimes referred to as *slots*) and in what order to ask for them.

Here's an example using the ever-popular pizza-ordering domain (did you know the average American eats about 46 slices of pizza each year?). The information slots that need to be acquired to successfully order a pizza include the following:

- Number of pizzas
- Size(s)
- Toppings
- Street address
- Phone number
- Zip code

Your VUI could force the user to go down the exact same path every time to get these, but a better way is to let the user provide the information the way they most want to:

> **PIZZA APP**
> Hi there, welcome to Pearl's Pizza, home of the famous gingerbread pizza crust. What kind of pizza can I get you?

USER
Um, I'd like a large pepperoni, please.

[At this point, we have filled in the number of pizzas (1), and the top-pings (pepperoni). Now, we know all that remains is the address and phone number.]

PIZZA APP
That's one large pepperoni. Great. What's the delivery address?

USER
Cherry Lane.

PIZZA APP
And the street number?

USER
321.

PIZZA APP
And finally, what's your zip code?

USER
94019.

Now let's see how another user might respond to this task:

PIZZA APP
Hi there, welcome to Pearl's Pizza, home of the famous gingerbread pizza crust. What kind of pizza can I get you?

USER
Uhh...yeah, I wanna order some pizzas.

PIZZA APP
Great, that's what I'm here for. How many would you like?

USER
Two, please.

PIZZA
And what sizes?

USER
One small, one large.

PIZZA APP
OK, let's start with the small. What ingredients would you like on that one?

USER

Olives, mushrooms, and sun-dried tomatoes.

PIZZA APP

Olives, mushrooms, sun-dried tomatoes. Sounds delicious. Now, what about the large; what ingredients would you like on that one?

In the second example, the user started out at a much higher level, but the pizza app successfully led them through the necessary questions to get the information. Follow your user's lead, and be prepared to handle information in a variety of ways.

Don't Leave Your User Hanging

One of the drawbacks of the current VUI technology is that there are a lot of big promises that can't always be met. Siri says, "What can I help you with?" inviting you to ask anything you want, when in fact, there is a constrained set of things she can handle. The Amazon Echo has no help screen, so when she doesn't understand you, it's not obvious what to do next.

But you can often still meet your user halfway. Alexa allows users to simply say, "Alexa, play some music," and, if you're an Amazon Prime member, she will say, "Here's a Prime Station you might like," and begin playing music. If Alexa understands you requested a song, but didn't understand which one, she will even suggest a particular music channel and start playing it.

Should the VUI Display What It Recognized?

Another design decision that you'll quickly need to make is whether to display what the user has said.

In most of the "assistant" VUIs out there today, what the user says is displayed on the phone screen, often in real time. It has become a standard in these use cases (though it was not always this way). Sometimes, displaying the recognition result is a good idea, and helpful to the user experience; other times, it's distracting.

For assistants such as Google, Siri, and Cortana, it can be helpful to see what the system recognized. The reason is that many times the response is simply turned into a search request, and if the assistant gets it wrong, you'd like to know. For example, if I say, "Please tell me the best restaurants in Paris," but it actually recognized "Please tell me the best *restrooms* in Paris," that's something I would like to know, so I don't end up eating in the restroom at the Eiffel Tower.

In a more conversational system, one in which the user is having a series of back-and-forths, displaying what the user said can be distracting and sometimes even have a negative impression.

As we have discussed earlier, speech recognition is not 100 percent accurate. It is accurate *enough* to be successful with many tasks, but nonetheless, it is often wrong. For example, I said to Google, "I'm just testing your speech recognition, you know I'm trying..." Figure 5-6 shows what it thought I said.

In the previous example of searching for information, if the VUI is providing me with search results, I need to know if it understood me—all of my words, which were carefully chosen, matter.

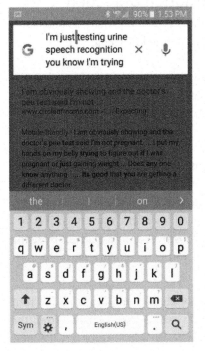

FIGURE 5-6.

Google misrecognized "I'm just testing your" as "I'm just testing urine"

In a more conversational VUI, getting every single word correct is not required to move forward in the conversation. As I discussed earlier in the chapter, a common misrecognition of the word "fine" is "find." When the system asks me how I'm doing and I reply, "fine," the system can easily add "find" as a possible key phrase match to "fine." The app can successfully handle it. But if the app also *displays* the result, right off the bat the user is going to be distracted by the misrecognition, which can result in a negative impression of the app's capability, even if it does the right thing and smoothly moves to the next turn in the conversation. This also applies to things such as names (having my name, "Cathy" recognized as "Kathy," for example), which people have emotional attachments to; there is no need to make them distrustful of the system in such cases.

In the conversational case, people often use more filler words around the key concepts, and it's not so important to get each of those absolutely right. If we recognized the main point of the user's response, we can move on successfully, and there is no need to alert the user to the fact that what they said was incorrectly recognized.

Sentiment Analysis and Emotion Detection

One way to make your VUI smarter and more empathetic is to use *sentiment analysis*. Sentiment analysis, as defined by Google, is:

> The process of computationally identifying and categorizing opinions expressed in a piece of text, especially in order to determine whether the writer's attitude towards a particular topic, product, etc., is positive, negative, or neutral.

In the VUI world, this means using natural-language processing to extract information about how the user is feeling. It might sound complicated, but you can begin to do basic sentiment analysis in a fairly straightforward manner. First, you need to define your categories. You can begin simply, for example, with "positive" and "negative." By using lists of positive and negative words, you can compare what the user said, and categorize accordingly.

There are even free word lists already created and available for your use, such as the MPQA negative and positive lists, available from the University of Pittsburgh (*http://mpqa.cs.pitt.edu/*). Open source tools such as KNIME can perform post-processing on your recognition results to examine what percent of the time your users are saying negative words versus positive words.

Emotion detection is still fairly new. Companies such as Affectiva have already begun using emotion detection techniques that look at a person's facial features. The company has employed this in market research; for example, while participants watch movie trailers, it tracks their facial features and determines their emotional response to various parts of the trailer.

Beyond Verbal detects emotions via a voice stream by analyzing vocal intonations in real time. With its Moodies app, users press a button and talk about their thoughts—after 20 seconds, the app displays their primary emotion, as shown in Figure 5-7.

FIGURE 5-7.
Beyond Verbal's Moodies app

One of the key principles to keep in mind when using technologies that deal with a user's emotion is to always err on the side of caution. Getting the user's emotional state right is great—getting it wrong can have a very high cost. Never come right out and name the user's emotion; for example, "You're feeling sad." Maybe the user is indeed feeling sad, maybe they aren't; but they might not want to admit it. We've all experienced saying to someone, "I can tell you're upset," only to have the person vehemently deny it.

Instead, use the sentiment and emotion analysis to *steer* the conversation. Perhaps someone has expressed negative emotions over multiple days this week when chatting with your VUI; the system could ask more questions, and dig a little deeper into how the person is actually feeling.

Text-to-Speech Versus Recorded Speech

Another important design decision is whether your VUI will use Text-to-Speech (TTS) or a recorded voice. The early days of interactive voice response (IVR) systems saw nearly 100 percent use of a recorded voice talent. TTS quality was not as good as it is today, and there were generally a fixed number of prompts the system could say.

Although TTS has improved in leaps and bounds, it's still not as understandable out of the box as a good voice talent. In addition, TTS has difficultly pronouncing certain words and can't always match the intonation you desire. Emotion is more difficult to project. For example, an experienced voice talent, when given the proper context, would know just how much emphasis to put into the phrase "Great!" Some TTS voices, when given this phrase, make it sound as if you've just won the lottery. Other TTS engines pronounce basic things like "OK" as "auk," causing unexpected behaviors.

On the downside, recording prompts does require more money and time up front. You need a recording studio, a good voice talent, and an audio engineer. In addition, when changes are needed, the voice talent must record new prompts.

TTS often has licensing fees, but it has the advantage of being easily changed. You can create new prompts on the fly. TTS is still somewhat limited; even Alexa will say, if you ask her how to pronounce something, "I say it like <x>, but text-to-speech is not always right."

TTS can be improved by applying Speech Synthesis Markup Language (SSML), which adds more natural pronunciations and intonation, but there are still words or phrases with which TTS engines will have difficulty. It might be necessary to build a pronunciation dictionary for your app so that it does not butcher common words in your app's domain.

Today's most sophisticated systems, such as Cortana, have a hybrid of human voices and TTS. Many of Cortana's prompts are recorded in full by the system's voice talent (Jen Taylor in the US version); other prompts are pieces of recordings, smoothly concatenated together. This also can be costly, but it combines the advantages of the human voice with the dynamic capabilities of TTS.

You can use a voice to signify other information, as well. For example, the Bay Area Rapid Transit (BART) system uses a male TTS voice when announcing trains coming from one direction, and a female voice for the other direction. It's a subtle cue most people are not even consciously aware of that still helps people know when to pay attention.

Even when recording a voice talent, concatenation strategies are important. It would be foolish, for example, to record every possible phone number out there. However, there is more to it than simply recording each number in insolation. Instead, each number must be recorded in three different ways. Here is an example for the phone number 650-555-1269, in which each digit must be recorded in three different ways by the voice actor:

- Midrange intonation (last digit in the area code and prefix: the 0 and the 5)

- Neutral intonation (all the other numbers, except the last 9)

- Falling intonation (the 9 at the end)

In addition, you should insert the appropriate pauses between the digit groups: about 200 milliseconds works well for phone numbers.

You have no doubt heard older IVR systems that don't employ this methodology; the phone number read back sounds stilted and slow.

You also can concatenate phrases. In the San Francisco Bay Area 511 IVR system, callers can get local traffic information, which includes reading out details of incidents and conditions, such as accidents or construction. The database that provided these details had each piece chunked into a category, including the road, the direction, the type of incident, and the duration. James Giangola and I developed a system to separate these pieces for the voice talent to record so that when concatenated, they sounded like complete, natural sentences.

Here's an example of a traffic incident:

As of 10:18 AM, there's a slowdown on highway 101 northbound, between Ralston Avenue in Belmont and Dore Avenue in San Mateo. Traffic is moving between 25 and 30 miles per hour.

These two sentences comprise the following 19 different pieces of recorded content:

As of
10
18
AM
there's a slowdown
on
Highway 101
northbound
between
Ralston Avenue
in Belmont
and
Dore Avenue
in San Mateo
Traffic is moving between
20
and
30
miles per hour

Recording this content does take a bit more work and planning up front, but in these types of situations, the payoff is worth it because the system sounds more natural.

For more details on the best way to do concatenation, refer to Jennifer Balogh's paper[2] as well as Chapter 11 of *Voice User Interfaces Design*.[3]

Another principle for creating the best VUI user experience includes not asking users for things before they're needed. This is the same as when designing a GUI: if you've created a shopping app, you might think it would be simplest to collect all the information you might need up front—name, address, and so on. But there is no need to bog down a user with extra input tasks until the point at which it's actually needed. Your user might simply be browsing and not necessarily planning to make a purchase. As Nass says, you would not ask a customer to hand over their credit card while they're wandering the store.[4]

Speaker Verification

Speaker verification (also known as voice biometric authentication) allows users to authenticate themselves by using just their voice. Back in the early 2000s, we used speaker verification to unlock building doors by picking up a phone next to the entryway and saying, "my voice is my password." We also used speaker verification to make long-distance phone calls (remember those?) through the company dialer.

Despite being around for a while, voice ID is not that widely used in consumer products today. Charles Schwab recently rolled out voice ID to authenticate account logins. Google also utilizes speaker verification by allowing you to record yourself saying "Ok Google" several times and then using that voiceprint to unlock your phone. The Google version is not as secure, however; my son can break into my account. Mattel has a diary called "My Password Journal" that allows its users to set up a password of their choice using their voices.

---

2   Balogh, J. "Strategies for Concatenating Recordings in a Voice User Interface: What We Can Learn From Prosody." Extended Abstracts, *CHI* (*Computer Human Interface*) (2001): 249–250.

3   Cohen, M., Giangola, J., and Balogh, J. *Voice User Interface Design.* (Boston, MA: Addison-Wesley, 2004), 6, 8, 75, 218, 247-248, 250-251, 259.

4   Nass, C., and Brave, S. *Wired for Speech.* (Cambridge, MA: The MIT Press, 2005), 181.

Passwords and passcodes are generally not advisable for VUIs, because anyone near you can hear what you're saying. Saying your banking password out loud is not secure, whereas a common pass phrase, such as "my voice is my password" doesn't rely on the words themselves.

Given the rise of password-alternatives such as fingerprint authentication on smartphones, it will be interesting to see whether speaker verification will become more or less popular. Recently a story was in the news about someone using a voice-enabled home assistant to unlock a neighbor's door by shouting at it from *outside* the house.

If you want to use speaker verification in your VUI system, you will need to license an engine (e.g., Nuance) that offers such technology. In addition, it will need a "voice enrollment" dialog to walk the user through the steps of setting up the authentication.

Another use for speaker verification—more relevant to our discussion of VUIs—applies not to authenticating a user for security, but rather speaker *identification*, so that the VUI can identify who in a particular conversation is speaking. A few companies have begun building systems to do this for transcribing meeting minutes.

"Wake" Words

Earlier in the book, we touched on the concept of a "wake" word. For example, saying "Alexa" to the Amazon Echo, or "Ok Google," to your Android device. A wake word is a handy way to start an interaction with a VUI system without having to physically touch the device. That's very useful for when you're across the room, driving, or have your hands covered in sticky pie dough.

Crafting an appropriate wake word is key. First, you want something easily recognizable, and not easily confusable. Something short, like "Bob," is too difficult to recognize on its own. It goes without saying that you should ensure your wake word is easy for people to say. Amazon allows you to choose one of three wake words: Alexa, Amazon, or Echo. Notice they are all multiple syllables. Finally, it's best not to choose a word that people might say commonly in conversations, to avoid waking up the device when not intended.

Amazon spent a lot of time tuning these to strike just the right balance between over-recognition (e.g., having it think you said "Alexa" when in fact you said "Alaska") and under-recognition (having to say "Alexa" 10 times because it's not quite sure that you really said it).

In addition, wake words should be handled locally. Your device/app will always need to be listening for its wake word; recording everything the user says, even when not engaged with your app, and sending it to the cloud is not ethical. Instead, it should be processed on the device or phone itself, and only when the wake word has been confidently recognized should your app begin streaming/recording the user's audio (which should of course be anonymized).

Context

One reason many virtual assistants (as well as chatbots) currently struggle with conversational UI is because they lack context. Context means being aware of what's going on around the conversation, as well as things that have happened in the past.

Remembering details of the conversation can be quite challenging, but one can still take advantage of basic context to make your VUI seem smarter as well as saving users' time.

For example, you can determine which time zone your user is in and greet them appropriately ("Good morning," "Good afternoon," etc.). You can use location; knowing that a user is at home and not at the office when they are searching for a restaurant will alter the search results you present.

If you ask your user every day how they slept, rather than act like the previous day never happened, alter the question with some background. Instead of "How many hours did you sleep last night?" the assistant could say, "I know you've been a bit short on sleep this week. How many hours were you able to get last night?"

Even within the same conversation, pay attention to things your user might say that are not responses to the direct question. If the user tells a tech support app, "My Internet hasn't been working for a week," don't follow up with, "How long has your Internet not been working?"

These are jarring reminders to the user that your system is just a dumb computer. Remembering that last week your user got their personal best time when they went for a run is not terribly difficult, computationally speaking. But knowing simple details like that will enable your VUI to engage the user more, to become more trusted, and more personable.

Advanced Multimodal

We've talked about combining the visual with the voice in terms of when to display content rather than speak it (such as a long list or a map) as well as allowing users to respond via touch or voice depending on the context. In addition, you can present speech confirmations via a visual medium (such as a button being highlighted) rather than confirming with speech every time the user speaks.

These types of strategies are done one at a time; the user speaks, and a visual result appears. The user taps a microphone icon, and then speaks.

What if the modes were combined in a way is already used by humans? For example, if I ask, "What's the capital of this state?" while pointing to Kansas on a map of the United States, anyone observing me will know which state I'm referring to. A VUI could do this as well by using the location of where the screen is tapped in conjunction with the speech input. For a chess game, for example, the user could tap a space while saying "move my knight here," or you could have a drawing program that combines the instruction "draw a flower" with the location at which the user tapped the canvas.

Another way to combine different modes is by switching smoothly between an agent and an app. The agent could direct the user to start a particular app on their phone, and during certain interactions, the user's speech would be directed to the app, such as saying an account number. This type of scenario is one way to help companies make their users more comfortable with doing transactions on their mobile devices, thus avoiding a call to human agents for certain tasks.

Bootstrapping Datasets

Chapter 2 briefly discusses building models of what user input your VUI will recognize. In some cases, you'll need to begin from scratch, building on your own knowledge and experience.

Whenever possible, it's best to bootstrap your initial models and key phrases. There are several sources for doing this.

WEBSITE DATA

If an existing website already has material related to your VUI app, terminology with which your users are familiar when referencing your product or service already exists. This is a great place to start. FAQs, customer service support forms—any way in which your users currently communicate via the web with the company. This includes transcripts from any chatbots the brand might have.

CALL CENTER DATA

In the IVR world, it's standard practice to obtain data from call centers, where users call in with questions or issues. Call center agents are a wealth of information; they know the problems with which customers really struggle.

DATA COLLECTION

In many cases, you might not have either of these resources available. Perhaps you're creating something brand new that has no alternative channel. In this case (and even if you do have the other resources), a great way to start off your dataset is by doing data collection.

Data collection involves asking people the questions the VUI would ask, and transcribing what people would say. Ideally, people contributing would be real users (or potential users) of your app. You can perform data collection in casual settings, or the setting can be more formalized. Although the best case is to simulate the same channel— having the users listen to the prompt and speak the response—typing their responses can still be valuable. One way to do this is via Amazon's Mechanical Turk. You can set up a task to play an audio file (or recording of your avatar) and then have workers respond to the prompt.

Although all of these methods are useful to begin building your models, keep in mind they are just that—the beginning. FAQs are not necessarily how people will state their questions. Typing is not always the same as talking. By the time your app has run its first pilot and collected real, in-the-wild data, you might find a lot of original data is no longer valid. Be prepared to let go of it. But it's still much better than starting from a blank slate.

Advanced NLU

A virtual assistant just doing a web search doesn't show understanding.

DEBORAH DAHL, MOBILE VOICE 2016

When confronted with a request they cannot answer, many virtual assistants will punt to a regular search command. Look at the difference between Siri and Hound when both are asked the question, "What is the population of Japan, and what is its capital?" Siri can't handle that question, so it backs off to, "OK, I found this on the web for 'What is the population of Japan and what is its capital?'" and shows a list of search results (Figure 5-8). Now, the first search result will actually give you all the information you need, but it does not answer the question directly.

FIGURE 5-8.

Siri goes to web search when it does not know the answer

In Hound's case, it says the answer right up front, and then provides additional information (Figure 5-9).

Hound has a knack for responding to multiple queries in one. Take a look at this doozy: "Show me coffee shops that have WiFi, are open on Sundays, and are within walking distance of my house." Hound can actually handle this quite gracefully (see Figure 5-10).

FIGURE 5-9.
An example of Hound handling a two-part question

FIGURE 5-10.
Hound handling a multipart request

This type of query draws a collective gasp when it's demonstrated before a live audience. It impresses people. But if you break it down, it's really just a series of simpler commands, concatenated.

Let's try something more complex: from an NLU perspective. When I ask Hound, "Who was president during the last World Series?" it backs off to search results. The first one? A page on Woodrow Wilson. This query is only asking for one piece of information—but it requires the underlying system to have a much more complex model of the world (Figure 5-11).

FIGURE 5-11.
Hound also backs off to search when it can't answer the question

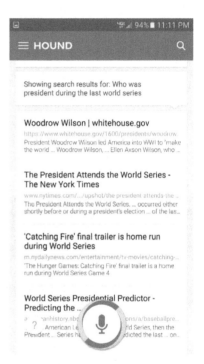

These examples show that VUI is not a solved problem. In all of these cases, the speech recognition was flawless. It recognized my question exactly. But that's not enough—in addition, the VUI must understand the subtleties of language.

What Hound does is very impressive—but that's generally not how people talk. If I call up a catalog company to order something, I give the information in chunks. Rather than saying, "I'd like to order a large men's shirt that is blue and has buttons and is short sleeved and is under $50," I'm more likely to begin with, "I'd like to order a men's shirt," and go from there. Your VUI will be most successful if it can *remember* what already took place, and keep the system grounded.

It might make for a more impressive investor meeting if you can demonstrate rattling off multiple commands at once, but users don't always mind if a task takes multiple steps. As long as the questions feel relevant, and the user feels like they're getting somewhere, they'll put up with a lot.

Another thing to keep in mind is that your user might give more information than you asked for. For example, you might think you're asking a simple yes/no question with, "Now, do you know the flight number?" But the user might give you "Yes" as well as "Yeah, it's 457." It's important to remember that people already have a host of rules of how to speak naturally, and we need to follow those:

> As designers, we don't get to create the underlying elements of conversation. [e.g., we must follow human conventions.][5]

In addition, spend time thinking about whether or not adding voice to the user's experience is actually helpful. As Randy Harris says:

> Voice enabling the Web for the sake of voice enabling the Web is pointless, but there are web sites galore with promise for useful speech interaction. The trick—provided there is a service with a potential customer base—is not to treat the web site itself as primary, but as the graphic interface to data the customer wants to access. It's the data, not the site, that is the key.[6]

5   Cohen, M., Giangola, J., and Balogh, J. *Voice User Interface Design.* (Boston, MA: Addison-Wesley, 2004), 6, 8, 75, 218, 247-248, 250-251, 259.

6   Harris, R. *Voice Interaction Design: Crafting the New Conversational Speech Systems.* (San Francisco, CA: Elsevier, 2005), 210.

Conclusion

To make your VUI perform above and beyond a basic exchange of information, take advantage of the concepts outlined in this chapter, such as allowing for more complex input by the user by going beyond simple keyword recognition.

Think carefully about design choices such as using TTS or a recorded voice. Use natural-sounding concatenation strategies to improve comprehension. Spend time outlining whether your VUI should have a wake word or require push-to-talk.

Make your VUI more successful out of the gate by bootstrapping your datasets with information that's already out there or by doing your own data collection.

Using all of these techniques will make your VUI easier to use, more accurate, and more successful.

[6]

User Testing for Voice User Interfaces

AS WITH ANY TYPE OF APPLICATION DESIGN, user testing is extremely important when creating voice user interfaces (VUIs). There are many similarities to testing regular mobile apps, but there are differences, as well. This chapter outlines practical ways (from cheap to more expensive) to get your VUI tested, how to interview your subjects, and how to measure success. It will enable VUI designers to immediately execute user testing at even early stages of development. It will focus primarily on VUI-specific methodologies.

Special VUI Considerations

Generally speaking, it is preferable not to reveal to the users at the start of testing that the system uses speech recognition up front (unless they would know this by the app description when downloading it in the real world, or from marketing). One of the important things to determine during testing is whether users understand that they can talk to the system. Do they know how, or when?

I have observed people failing to speak when speech was allowed because it was not at all obvious that they *could* speak. Some of these users later commented, "I sure wish I could speak there!" Obviously, the design needed some work, but I might not have discovered this had I explicitly informed them that they could always speak to the app from the outset.

A common strategy with GUI testing is asking people to narrate what they're doing, which obviously won't work when testing a real VUI system.

If you already have experience in conducting other types of usability testing and want to jump straight into the more VUI-focused portion of this chapter, skip ahead to "Things to Look For" on page 173.

Background Research on Users and Use Cases

As with any type of design, conducting user research in the early stages is highly recommended. Although we will summarize a few basic principles of user research, you can learn more about it from sources dedicated to the subject. O'Reilly Media has an abundance of user research video tutorials available online, which you can access at *http://bit.ly/user-research-fundamentals-lp*.

DON'T REINVENT THE WHEEL

One of the first questions to ask during your research phase is whether something similar to what you're developing has already been done, albeit in a different way. For example, perhaps you are creating a mobile app for a service that already exists as a website. It's important to examine what already exists to learn what works (or doesn't). For VUI systems in particular, an interactive voice response (IVR) system version often already exists (sometimes DTMF [touch tone] only, and sometimes voice-enabled). This is a great place to discover what similar features are already out there and how they are handled.

Mobile VUIs should never be an exact replica of their IVR counterparts, but it is still possible to learn a lot from them, such as how concepts are grouped and which ones are used most frequently.

If there is a similar IVR system out there, it often means there is a human agent supporting it, and therefore a call center. Sitting in a call center for an afternoon listening in on calls can provide a wealth of information. Listening to real users call in can reveal things that a study of just the IVR system itself might not identify.

In addition, interviewing call center agents can also provide a huge amount of valuable information. They are the ones who know what users are really calling in about, what the biggest complaints are, and what information can be difficult for callers to find.

But perhaps you're designing a mobile app that has no IVR component. What problem does your VUI solve? What real-world things exist that might help you gain insights?

Cortana, for example, is a virtual assistant. For inspiration, Microsoft interviewed real-life personal assistants. Designers found that human assistants often needed to ask for help when they did not understand an assigned task. Therefore, Microsoft made sure to have Cortana ask for help if she needs it, just like her human counterparts.[1]

In addition, real personal assistants often carry around a notebook about the person they're assisting; Cortana maintains a similar notebook.

Always interview people who are in the space you're trying to serve. As an example, a company I was consulting for had decided to create a VUI app about Parkinson's disease. The original idea was an app to help people *with* Parkinson's, providing more information about the disease, helping with medication management, and other self-care tasks. When conducting user research, I also wanted to speak to those closest to Parkinson's patients: their caregivers. When I did so, I realized that an equally important problem was helping the caregivers themselves! It modified the direction and feature set we had planned for building the app. I also reached out to support groups for both Parkinson's patients and their caregivers. This goes without saying, but be respectful and transparent when conducting your user research—people are often willing to talk, and want to help, but be open about what you're try-ing to accomplish. Don't dismiss people's ideas—you're not making a promise to implement them, but you need to listen closely to the issues people are dealing with.

Designing a Study with Real Users

Testing with real users, early and often, is crucial. After your app is out there, it is much more difficult to change the user experience (UX) than it is earlier, during design and development. As designers, it's easy to view your app through your own lens of desires and experiences. Having other people test will open your eyes to things that might never have occurred to you otherwise. As an example, when showing an early version of our mobile app from Sensely, I discovered that many people

---

1   Weinberger, M. (2016). "Why Microsoft Doesn't Want Its Digital Assistant, Cortana, to Sound Too Human." Retrieved from *http://businessinsider.com/*.

had no idea that they could scroll down to see more items in a list. We were so used to using the app ourselves, it didn't occur to us, but we quickly realized we had to modify the design.

TASK DEFINITION

Whether doing early-stage testing, trying out a prototype, or conducting a full-blown usability test on a working system, it's important to carefully define the tasks you'll request your users to perform. As introduced in the book *Voice User Interface Design*:

> In a typical usability test, the participant is presented with a number of tasks, which are designed to exercise the parts of the system you wish to test. Given that it is seldom possible to test a system exhaustively, the tests are focused on primary dialog paths (e.g., features that are likely to be used frequently), tasks in areas of high risk, and tasks that address the major goals and design criteria identified during requirements definition.
>
> You should write the task definitions carefully to avoid biasing the participant in any way. You should describe the goal of the task without mentioning command words or strategies for completing the task.[2]

Be careful when writing your task: you want to avoid giving away too much and instead provide just the essential information. As Harris says, "the scenario needs only a hint of plot."[3] Describe tasks in the way users would talk about them—don't use technical terms, or things that give away key commands.

Harris suggests making the early tasks "relatively simple, even trivial, to put the participants at ease."[4]

Jennifer Balogh, coauthor of *Voice User Interface Design*, stresses the importance of task order, and that to avoid ordering effects, it's best to randomize them:

---

2   Cohen, M., Giangola, J., and Balogh, J. *Voice User Interface Design*. (Boston, MA: Addison-Wesley, 2004), 6, 8, 75, 218, 247-248, 250-251, 259.

3   Harris, R. *Voice Interaction Design: Crafting the New Conversational Speech Systems*. (San Francisco, CA: Elsevier, 2005), 489.

4   Harris, *Voice Interaction Design*, 474.

Order effects can happen. So, if you have everyone in a study go through all the tasks in the same order, one task can influence the behavior in later tasks. I experienced this in one study in which the task was to have the subject ask for an agent. After the subject did this, on subsequent tasks, the subjects were more likely to ask for an agent. This command wouldn't have occurred to them otherwise (when the agent task was not before other tasks, the subjects did not ask for an agent). The solution (although time consuming) is to rotate the tasks across subjects. One way to do this is with a technique called Latin Square design.

A *Latin Square* design allows you to present each task in every position and have each task follow every other task without having to go through every permutation. For example, 5 tasks would result in 120 permutations. In a Latin Square design, there would only be five conditions, as presented in Table 5-1.

TABLE 5-1. Latin Square design

	TASK 1	TASK 2	TASK 3	TASK 4	TASK 5
Subject 1	A	B	E	C	D
Subject 2	B	C	A	D	E
Subject 3	C	D	B	E	A
Subject 4	D	E	C	A	B
Subject 5	E	A	D	B	C

You can find more on Latin Square design by searching online.

CHOOSING PARTICIPANTS

As with all user testing, it's best to sample subjects who are in the demographics of the people for whom you're actually designing the system. If you are creating a health app for people with chronic heart failure, your test subjects should not be healthy college students. The further away from the true demographic your subjects are, the less reliable the results will be.

How many people should you test? If you get the right demographics, you don't need that many. Usability expert Jakob Nielsen recommends five users for most types of testing. The reason five is enough? Here's how he explains it:

> The vast majority of your user research should be qualitative; that is, aimed at collecting insights to drive your design, not numbers to impress people in PowerPoint. The main argument for small tests is simply return on investment: testing costs increase with each additional study participant, yet the number of findings quickly reaches the point of diminishing returns. There's little additional benefit to running more than five people through the same study; ROI drops like a stone with a bigger N.[5]

Recruiting users can be tough. There are companies that can help you find subjects, but their costs are often prohibitive for smaller companies. If your company is large enough to afford a recruiting firm, it's a very effective way to get users in the right demographic. Recruiting companies will require a "screener," a document outlining the qualifications you need for your users. Questions might include age range, what type of smartphone they own, their level of expertise with certain apps, their geographic location, or anything else to ensure the right demographics.

[NOTE]

For more on screeners, check out the User Testing Blog at *https://www.usertesting.com/blog/2015/01/29/screener-questions/*.

For some testing, it's also appropriate to recruit friends and family. That can be a great way to do some quick and dirty testing and get feedback on crucial aspects quickly.

Remote testing widens the net because you can recruit people who aren't local. For quick and affordable testing, services such as Task Rabbit can identify people to do your study, although you can't choose the demographics. There are also online services such as UserTesting

---

5   Neilsen, J. (2012). "How Many Test Users in a Usability Study?" Retrieved from *https://www.nngroup.com/*.

(*https://usertesting.com/*) and UserBob (*https://userbob.com/*), both of which have a pool of users available for testing. There are some technical hurdles, however, as the screen capture software used is not always able to capture both the app's audio (e.g., the virtual assistant speaking) as well as the user's speech, and the user's screen. You can overcome this by having the user record the session using a webcam to record the session, but this will limit the pool of users and can add to the cost of user payment, as well.

Be sure to compensate your subjects. Local subjects who come to you for in-person testing should generally be paid more. Subjects who represent very specific demographic groups will also have a higher rate.

QUESTIONS TO ASK

The questions you ask are crucial to gaining insights from your user testing. Observational data is important, but the right questions can tease out important pieces of the user's experience. In addition, subjects tend to skew on the positive side, especially during face-to-face sessions—most people want to be nice and will sometimes hesitate to provide negative feedback, or exaggerate the positive. It's often unconscious, but a good interviewer can get past these issues.

Beware of priming your subjects when giving instructions. As Harris notes, when it comes to what to say, users take substantial cues from the person conducting the testing.[6]

If possible, ask subjects a few questions after each task, and then a set of questions at the very end. The reason for this is because subjects might forget things as they move from task to ask. The best time to ask about first impressions is right after the very first task is completed.

Avoid leading the subject—let them explain in their own words. If a subject asks, "Could I have spoken to the app during that task?" you should first ask, "Would you want to do that?" If the subject says, "I didn't like it," don't say, "Oh, because it didn't understand when you said 'show me my shopping list'"?" Instead, say, "Tell me more about that." Do more listening and less talking. Pauses are OK; sometimes you'll be typing or writing notes, and the user will add more information on her own.

---

6 Harris, R. *Voice Interaction Design: Crafting the New Conversational Speech Systems.* (San Francisco, CA: Elsevier, 2005), 489.

When you begin testing, remind participants that they're not being tested, but that they are there to help improve the system, and that you won't be offended by their feedback. Don't interrupt when you see them struggling, unless they become too frustrated to continue.

For quantitative questions, the Likert scale is commonly used. Here are some good guidelines about using Likert, L., and Algina, J.:[7]

- Put statements or questions in the present tense.

- Do not use statements that are factual or capable of being interpreted as factual.

- Avoid statements that can have more than one interpretation.

- Avoid statements that are likely to be endorsed by almost everyone or almost no one.

- Try to have an almost equal number of statements expressing positive and negative feelings.

- Statements should be short, rarely exceeding 20 words.

- Each statement should be a proper grammatical sentence.

- Statements containing universals such as "all," "always," "none," and "never" often introduce ambiguity and you should avoid them.

- Avoid the use of indefinite qualifiers such as "only," "just," "merely," "many," "few," or "seldom."

- Whenever possible, statements should be in simple sentences rather than complex or compound sentences. Avoid statements that contain "if" or "because" clauses.

- Use vocabulary that the respondents can easily understand.

- Avoid the use of negatives (e.g., "not", "none," "never").

Table 6-1 presents a sample questionnaire, created by Jennifer Balogh at Intelliphonics, that you should ask at the very end of an in-person user testing session.

---

7   Crocker, L. and Algina, J. *Introduction to Classical and Modern Test Theory.* (Mason, Ohio: Cengage Learning, 2008), 80.

TABLE 6-1. Likert questionnaire

Please rate the system you just experienced. Read each statement and decide how much you agree or disagree with the statement. The choices range from "strongly disagree" to "strongly agree." Use one check mark per statement.

	(1) STRONGLY DISAGREE	(2) DISAGREE	(3) SOMEWHAT DISAGREE	(4) NEUTRAL	(5) SOMEWHAT AGREE	(6) AGREE	(7) STRONGLY AGREE
The system is easy to use.							
I like the flow of the video.							
The system understands what I say.							
Sometimes the advice seems irrelevant.							
It is fun to play around with the system.							
The idea of talking to a video strikes me as strange.							
The system is confusing.							
I find the system entertaining.							

	(1) STRONGLY DISAGREE	(2) DISAGREE	(3) SOMEWHAT DISAGREE	(4) NEUTRAL	(5) SOMEWHAT AGREE	(6) AGREE	(7) STRONGLY AGREE
The video is too choppy.							
The conversation feels very canned to me.							
I am happy with the advice offered.							
I will try to avoid using this system in the future.							
It feels like I am having a conversation with someone.							
I like the idea of being able to interact like this.							
I would be happy to use the system again and again.							

The questionnaire consisted of questions that probed seven different dimensions of the application (labeled categories): accuracy, concept, advice offered (content), ease of use, authenticity of the conversation, likability, and video flow. For each category, the questionnaire included both a positively phrased statement such as, "I like the flow of the video," and a negatively phrased statement such as, "The video is too choppy." Because likability was of interest in the study, three additional positively phrased statements covering this category were included in the questionnaire.

Open responses (to be asked verbally)

Thinking about the system overall, what did you like the most about it?

How did you think the system could be improved?

Note that negatively phrased statements ("The system is confusing") are used along with positively phrased statements ("The system is easy to use.")

This is important so as not to bias users. As indicated previously, subjects are often more positive when being interviewed than they might be on their own. In addition, I find that asking negative questions causes people to stop and think a bit more about the answer, because it throws them off slightly and they need to reframe their thinking.

In this example, the questions are grouped into similar categories, with a score calculated for each aspect. To allow for direct comparisons between positive and negative statements, answers to negatively phrased statements are reversed such that a response of 1 is mapped onto a score of 7, 2 is mapped onto 6, and so on.

An average score for each of the seven categories was calculated. Here is how the categories (and scores) for this particular user test turned out (using similar questions):

Video Flow	6.00
Ease of Use	5.67
Advice Offered (Content)	4.83
Accuracy	4.75
Likability	4.73
Concept	4.42
Authenticity of Conversation	3.75

These were summarized more quantitatively by Balogh and her assistant (Lalida Sritanyaratana) in the report itself. Here are some of the conclusions:

- The highest rated area of the app was the flow of the video. In debriefing, participants had positive comments about the video. Participant 4 said, "I like the way the video flows." Participant 5 said the "video was smooth." The other high scoring area was ease of use. Some comments from debriefing corroborated this finding. Participants often said that the app was simple, clear, and easy to use.

- The lowest scoring dimension of the application was the authenticity of the conversation. Participants realized that there were planned responses for all the various responses to the app. Participant 3 said that phrases like, "Sorry, I didn't catch that," sounded ingenuine to him. Participant 4 said, "It's OK, but I know the answers are canned." Similarly, Participant 6 said, "I know that it's prerecorded."

- For general likability, most participants agreed that they "liked the app." For this question, Participant 6 was neutral, Participants 3 and 4 somewhat agreed and Participants 1, 2, and 5 agreed. So, the majority of the responses to this question were positive. The average score of 5.33 (where 5 was "somewhat agree") was the third highest score on any of the questions on the survey. However, some improvement is needed to reach a likability threshold of 5.5.

THINGS TO LOOK FOR

While observing your subjects (or looking at videos of remote testing), it's important to take note of not just what the users did or did not do in the app, but facial expressions and body language. Did they laugh in a place that was unexpected? Did they frown when asked a particular question by the app?

Here are some other things to look for when conducting usability testing of a VUI:

- Do your users know when they can speak and when they can't—that is, do they know that speech is allowed, and if so, do they know *when* they can begin speaking?

- If you're doing early-stage testing, before the speech recognition is in place, what do they say? How realistic is it to be able to capture?

- Where are they confused and hesitant?

- Task duration: how long do users needs to complete the task?

If your user asks "What should I do now?" or "Should I press this button?", don't answer directly. Gently encourage the user to do whatever they might try when alone. If the app crashes or the user is becoming too frustrated, step in.

Early-Stage Testing

It's never too early to begin testing your concepts. In addition to traditional methods used to test mobile devices, UX researchers of VUIs often have some other low-fidelity approaches.

SAMPLE DIALOGS

One of the first steps for early-stage testing of VUIs, after the initial concepts have been determined, is to create sample dialogs. As you might remember from Chapter 2, a sample dialog is a conversation between the VUI and the user. It's not meant to be exhaustive, but it should showcase the most common paths as well as rarer but still important paths such as error recovery.

A sample dialog looks like a movie script, with the system and the user taking turns having a dialog.

Here's a sample dialog for an app that allows the user (a child) to have a conversation with the big man himself, Santa Claus. This was written by Robbie Pickard while at Volio.

TALK TO SANTA CLAUS

SANTA CLAUS sits in a big red chair, facing the USER. The toy factory is behind him—it's a busy scene.

SANTA CLAUS
Ho! Ho! Ho! Merry Christmas, little one! Welcome to the North Pole! What's your name?

USER
Claudia.

SANTA CLAUS
That's a lovely name. And how old are you?

USER
I'm seven.

SANTA CLAUS
Seven! That's great. The big day isn't too far away. Are you excited for Christmas?

USER
Yes!

SANTA CLAUS
So am I!

MRS. CLAUS brings Santa some milk and cookies.

MRS. CLAUS
Here you go, Santa; I brought you some milk and cookies.

SANTA CLAUS
Thank you, dear.

Santa holds up the two cookies for the user to see. One is chocolate chip and one is a sugar cookie with white frosting in the shape of a snowman.

(TO USER)

These look delicious...perhaps you can help me. Which one should I eat, the chocolate chip or the snowman?

USER

Eat both of them!

SANTA CLAUS (CHUCKLING)

My, oh my...that's a lot of cookies, but as you wish!

Santa takes a big bite of both cookies in quick succession, washing it down with a glass of milk.

SANTA CLAUS (CONTINUES)

Well those were delicious! As you can tell, I love Mrs. Claus's cookies!

(PATTING HIS BELLY)

You know, the elves and I are hard at work making toys for everyone. I gotta ask you: have you been naughty or nice this year?

USER

I've been nice!

SANTA CLAUS

Good for you! What's one nice thing you did this year?

USER

I helped my Mommy clean my room!

SANTA CLAUS

Well, that is nice of you.

Santa gets out a scroll and begins writing on it.

SANTA CLAUS

I'm going to put you on the Nice List. So now for the big question: what do you want for Christmas?

USER

I want a skateboard and a backpack!

SANTA CLAUS (JOLLY AS EVER)

Well, I think that should fit on my sleigh! Don't forget to leave me some cookies and milk!

THE END

When you have a few sample dialogs written up, do some "table reads" with other people. One person reads for the VUI, and one for the user. How does it sound? Is it repetitive? Stilted?

Do a table read with your developers, as well. You might have some items in your design (such as handling pronouns or referring to a user's previous behavior) that will take more complex development, and it's important to get buy-in from the outset and not surprise them late in the game.

One common finding from table reads is having too many transitions with the same wording; for example, saying "thank you" or "got it" three times in a row.

MOCK-UPS

As with any type of mobile design, mock-ups are a great way to test the look-and-feel of your app in the early stages. If you have an avatar, a mock-up is a good first start to get user's reactions to how the avatar looks, even if it's not yet animated, and even if speech recognition is not yet implemented.

WIZARD OF OZ TESTING

Pay no attention to that man behind the curtain!
THE GREAT AND POWERFUL OZ

Wizard of Oz (WOz) testing occurs when the thing being tested does not yet actually exist, and a human is "behind the curtain" to give the illusion of a fully working system.

WOz testing comes early. According to Harris, WOz testing is a "part of the creative process of speech-system design, not a calibration instrument for an almost-finished model developed at arm's length from the users."[8]

To conduct WOz testing, you will need two researchers: the Wizard, and an assistant. The Wizard will generally be focused on listening to the user and enabling the next action, so this same person cannot be the one responsible for interviewing and note taking.

---

8   Harris, R. *Voice Interaction Design: Crafting the New Conversational Speech Systems.* (San Francisco, CA: Elsevier, 2005).

When I was at Nuance Communications, WOz testing was a common and low-cost way to test IVR systems before they were built. Because users were interacting over the phone, it was easy to simulate a real IVR system. We created a web-based tool that had a list of currently available prompts (including error prompts) in each step of the conversation, and the "wizard" would click on the appropriate prompt, which would then play out over the phone line.

We still had to design the flow and record the prompts, but no system code had to be written—just some simple HTML files (see Figure 6-1 for an example).

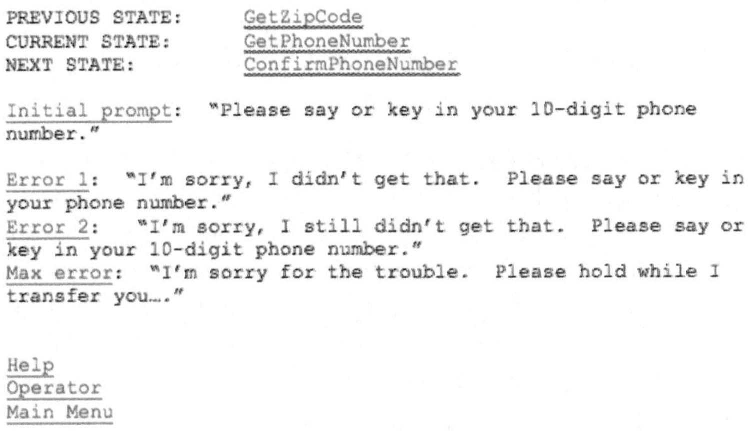

```
PREVIOUS STATE:     GetZipCode
CURRENT STATE:      GetPhoneNumber
NEXT STATE:         ConfirmPhoneNumber

Initial prompt:  "Please say or key in your 10-digit phone
number."

Error 1:  "I'm sorry, I didn't get that.  Please say or key in
your phone number."
Error 2:   "I'm sorry, I still didn't get that.  Please say or
key in your 10-digit phone number."
Max error:  "I'm sorry for the trouble.  Please hold while I
transfer you...."


Help
Operator
Main Menu
```

FIGURE 6-1.
WOz screen for IVR testing

Conducting WOz testing on a mobile app is trickier, because it's much more difficult to control remotely. Nonetheless, gathering user data before you have a fully working prototype can be valuable. Here are a few ways to do this type of testing before you have a working app:

Use texting

Although this will not simulate speech recognition, it can give you a picture of overall conversational flow and what types of things users might say. For this method, tell the user that they'll be texting with your new bot. Unbeknownst to the user, however, a human is on the other end. This could be done very easily by simply texting her with the opening prompt, and going from there.

Focus on an abbreviated task

In certain cases, you might simply be trying to learn what it is users think they can say in a given situation. For example, if you're trying to design a virtual assistant, your app can ask the question "What can I help you with?" and collect user responses, even if that's as far as it goes. No actual speech recognition is needed—just a mock-up of the screen and the prompt.

Always error-out

Another technique that you can use before your speech recognition is fully in place is to error-out. For example, if your app asks the user, "How many people will you be traveling with?" on any response, go into your back-off behavior, which could be something like, "I'm sorry, how many people?" and provide a GUI option (such as buttons). You'll still learn some valuable ways in which people interact with the system.

Test the GUI, even if the VUI is not ready

Because mobile VUI apps are often a combination, you can still test a variety of GUI elements by using tools such as Axure and InVision. These allow you to create a simple working model of a mobile app with just mock-ups, in which the user can swipe and press buttons to cause certain behaviors to occur. Axure also allows your prototype to play audio.

Although one advantage of WOz is the ability to test an early prototype, the other advantage is that it's much cheaper to make design changes before you've written most of the code than later on in the development cycle.

DIFFERENCE BETWEEN WOZ AND USABILITY TESTING

There is one major difference between WOz and usability testing when working with VUIs, and that is recognition accuracy.

When conducting WOz on a GUI, it's usually quite clear *where* the user has clicked the screen, or what part they've swiped or tapped. There's no ambiguity; you know that as soon as that button or list is hooked up to real code, it will do what is expected.

With VUI and natural-language interfaces, the Wizard has to do some on-the-fly interpretation and determine whether that's something we could realistically recognize. Sometimes it's easy and what the user said is quite obviously in-grammar. But other times it's more complex and the Wizard must make a snap judgment call to decide what the user really meant and whether it could be handled.

It's better to be on the conservative side as a Wizard, but don't worry too much—the testing will still do a good job capturing early issues.

Usability Testing

Usability testing refers to the stage when you have a working app. The system should have all of the features you want to test in a fully working state. If you need to test anything requiring personal information, such as a user profile or user search history, you will need to create a fake account. If the backend is still not hooked up, you can even test with hardcoded information.

Usability testing is not generally aimed at test recognition accuracy; it's meant to test the flow and ease of use. However, recognition issues can cause problems and prevent users from completing tasks. If possible, run a couple of sample subjects first to try to catch any major recognition issues and fix them before running the full study. That being said, recognition issues are still an important lesson to be learned. If there are particular places where your users have problems because they're not being recognized, that is clearly an issue that needs addressing.

Traditional usability testing takes place in a lab, but that's not the only way to run a successful usability test.

REMOTE TESTING

Some researchers still frown on remote usability testing, but it can be extremely effective if you do it correctly. Advantages to remote testing include the following:

- Easier to find people in your demographic because they do not need to be local

- Generally cheaper because people do not need to be paid for traveling to your site

- Better for testing "in the wild"—more similar to real-world scenarios

- Users are often less self-conscious, because no one is staring at them as they engage in the test

- Can be moderated or unmoderated—testing can occur without you being present

Moderated versus unmoderated

As just mentioned, remote testing allows for more flexibility in terms of the tester's participation. With remote testing, it's still possible to observe and interview subjects remotely by using video conferencing, or even the phone. Moderated testing means that as you watch participants, you can ask questions based on their actions, and probe for more details when their replies are sparse.

However, remote testing also allows the testing to occur when you are *not* present, which means testers can be free to perform the tasks at the time that's best for them. Unmoderated remote testing can still be a very effective way to conduct usability studies.

Video recording

Because you obviously will not be there in person during a remote usability test, you need to come up with a way to record what's going on with the user. When testing mobile apps with no audio component, using a screen recording app on a phone can do the trick, but it's more difficult when the app is speaking and the user is speaking to the app.

Some companies offer a service wherein some of their users have their own webcams and are comfortable recording testing sessions. This can become expensive, however, and limit your demographics to people who own and are able to use a webcam or other recording device.

When I was at Volio, we were already recording users' audio and video with our picture-in-picture feature on the iPad (users could see themselves in the corner, as they do in FaceTime), as shown in Figure 6-2. For remote testing, we simply left the recording on even when it was not the user's turn to speak, to capture any facial expressions and other audio. (We of course obtained their permission to do so, and kept the data internal.)

FIGURE 6-2.
When using the Volio app, users' video can be recorded, which is useful for user testing

This methodology proved to be remarkably effective. In addition to capturing what users were saying to the app during their turn, we were also observing their reactions to the content being presented to them. For example, when testing our stand-up comedian interactive app, while the comedian was telling a joke, we could observe the users' expressions—were they laughing? Bored? Offended?

After having users do several tasks, they completed a survey, which provided us with information about their subjective perceptions of the system. One downside to this type of remote testing is that you cannot follow-up on participants' responses in real time (unless of course you're testing an IVR system), but the benefits can often outweigh the disadvantages.

Services for remote testing

When conducting usability tests, sometimes you need to get creative, especially if you're at a small company with no real budget for user testing.

Another method for conducting remote user testing is to find a group of testers by using services such as Amazon's Mechanical Turk. "Workers" sign up for Mechanical Turk, and "Requesters" create tasks that can be done online via a web page. Workers can choose which tasks they want to do, and requesters pay them. Figure 6-3 presents an example of what a Mechanical Turk worker would see when performing a task.[9]

FIGURE 6-3.
Sample task for Amazon Mechanical Turk

Ann Thyme-Gobbel, currently VUI design lead at D+M Holdings, has successfully used Mechanical Turk to test comparisons of text-to-speech (TTS) versus recorded prompts. She asked Turkers to listen to various prompts that were happy, discouraging, disappointing, and other emotions, and then asked follow-up questions about trust and likability.

---

9 This example is taken from Amazon's "How to Create a Project" documentation (*http://docs.aws.amazon.com/AWSMechTurk/latest/RequesterUI/CreatingaHITT emplate.html*).

She feels remote testing has a variety of advantages over lab testing, and not just the fact that people are not required to come in to a lab. Remote testing can make it easier to simulate scenarios "in the wild." An example she gives is asking a user to refill a prescription over the phone. You can ask the remote user to find a real pill bottle in their house and read off the prescription number. Having them walk around the house while on the phone and looking for it will provide a much more realistic example of what it's like to do this task than to bring them into a lab and hand them a bottle.

When conducting user studies for their voice-enabled cooking app "Yes, Chef," Conversant Labs made sure to test in people's kitchens while they made real recipes, to ensure that the app would understand the way people really speak while cooking.

In addition, Thyme-Gobbel says that during remote testing:

> Participants share more. If you are sitting in the room with the participant, they're more likely to say, "You saw what happened," than to describe what they thought happened in some situation.

Remember to pay your subjects well, even with outsourcing. Mechanical Turk can be a much more affordable method than recruiting people yourself, but that doesn't mean you should not pay fairly. These methods also mean that your budget can be stretched further, so you can recruit more subjects. The rule of thumb of 5 to 10 usability subjects applies when the subjects are all in the appropriate demographic; if you have less control, you'll need more subjects.

LAB TESTING

Traditional usability testing is often done in a lab, with one-way mirrors and recording equipment. Recruiting subjects to do in-person testing can be very effective. Having recording equipment already set up is a great way to reliably record what's needed. The pros of lab testing include having a dedicated space to perform user testing (particularly important when you need a quiet place to do VUI testing), and the ability to have permanent recording equipment set up, allowing the user to do a task without the tester sitting right next to them and possibly making them uncomfortable (assuming a one-way mirror).

Some cons include the price, both of having and maintaining the lab as well as the cost of paying subjects to keep appointments and show up in person. It can also limit the demographic if the people you need are not available in your area.

There are of course variations in "lab" testing: you do not necessarily need a dedicated space, a particularly difficult thing to come by in a small company. A private quiet room can do just fine. Ideally, you will have a camera showing you what the user is seeing, so you do not need to sit too closely to observe.

GUERRILLA TESTING

When you don't have a budget for user testing, sometimes you need to simply go out into the world and ask people to try your app. Coffee shops, shopping malls, parks—any of these can be effective places to recruit subjects for on-the-fly testing. Be well armed with your mobile device, task definition, questions, and a reward. Homemade cookies, Starbucks gift cards, even stickers can be enough motivation for people to spend 5 to 15 minutes trying out your app. Remind them they're helping design a better app and that their feedback will help others.

Performance Measures

Collecting a combination of objective and subjective measurements is recommended. This combination is important because one measurement does not always give the full story. For example, perhaps the user completed the task successfully, but did not like something about it. Or, they might technically *not* be successful in their task, but not be bothered.

As Balogh explains, "you can find that subjects failed, but they didn't mind." I noticed this during Volio usability testing: in some cases, users' speech would not be correctly recognized, but because the error handling was relatively pain-free, users would not mark the app more negatively because of it. If I had only been marking down error counts, the results would have been different.

For objective measures, remember to tally observations and not just rely on impressions. Balogh says:

> Sometimes you will find that one subject made an impression on you, but when you actually count the instances of a behavior, the conclusion is different from what this one person experienced.

She cites a study that found five key measurements for testing VUI systems: accuracy and speed, cognitive effort, transparency/confusion, friendliness, and voice.[10]

Decide beforehand what "task completion" means for each task. If the user gets partway through a task but quits before it's finished, it could still be considered complete. For example, if the user is looking up their nearest pharmacy, but fails to click on the link to a map, it is still successful—perhaps the user only wanted to know the hours the pharmacy was open. If the user does end the task (voluntarily or not), follow up to ask if they believe they accomplished what was needed and, if not, why not.

Tracking the number and type of errors is very important in a VUI system. A rejection error, for example, is different than a mismatch (in which the user was incorrectly recognized as saying something else). In addition, it's important to note what happened after the error: did the user recover? How long did it take?

Next Steps

After you have run your subjects, tally up their responses to questions, their task completion rates, and number and types of errors.

Identify pain points. Where did the users struggle? Did they know when it was OK to speak? Where did they become lost—or impatient? When things did go wrong, were they able to recover successfully?

Write up your observations, and make a list of recommendations. Rank the issues by severity and share this with the entire team to create a plan on when and how you'll be able to fix them.

---

10 Larsen, L.B. (2003). "Assessment of spoken dialogue system usability: What are we really measuring?" Eurospeech, Geneva.

Testing VUIS in Cars, Devices, and Robots

When testing a VUI in contexts other than an IVR or mobile app, some differences apply.

CARS

Testing in the car is challenging. Large car companies and some universities have driving simulators, but for smaller companies it can be difficult to fund such equipment. Lower-cost options can include a mock-up of a car, with a monitor displaying a driving simulator, along with a steering wheel and holder for a phone or tablet for the driving app itself.

Lisa Falkson, lead voice UX designer at electric car company NEXTEV, often runs car usability testing in a real car, but while the car is stopped in a parking lot. This allows her to gain valuable information about how the user interacts with the system, their level of distraction, and what they can and cannot accomplish—in a much safer environment than if the user were actually driving.

Karen Kaushansky, director of experience at self-driving car company Zoox, reminds us that you don't need to have a fully working prototype to do initial experience testing. While at Microsoft, working on the Ford SYNC system (which allowed users to push a button and ask for their commute time, among other features), she used a low-fidelity method to do WOz testing.

The car did not yet have its push-to-talk button, so they attached a foam one to the steering wheel (Figure 6-4). While sitting in the parking lot, the Wizard sat in the backseat with a laptop, playing prompts that would, in the future, come from the car! Subjects were quickly caught up in the experience, allowing the team to do useful initial testing to discover things such as how people would ask for information about traffic.

FIGURE 6-4.
Ford SYNC prototype with foam "push-to-talk" button (with permission from K. Kaushansky)

DEVICES AND ROBOTS

Kaushansky talks about ways to test other devices, as well, not just cars, in the early stages, which she calls "experience prototyping." Suppose that you're building a smartwatch, but it will be a while before the first model exists. Even before that happens, you can test what it would be like to have such a device—strap one on your wrist and walk around the mall, talking to it. As Kaushansky says, "be Dick Tracy and put your mouth near your watch and say, 'What's the weather tomorrow?'"

As Tom Chi said in his TED talk in 2012 about rapid prototyping Google Glass, "Doing is the best kind of thinking." In other words, you can think long and hard about how people *might* interact with your device, but nothing beats having people *actually* interact with it (even in a crude prototype form).

If you're testing a device such as an Amazon Echo–type system, you can rig something up to do WOz testing, because all you need to do is play back prompts through the device. Imagine a scenario in which the user is in a room with the device, and the Wizard sits in the other room at the computer, ready to play prompts in response to the user's queries.

You can even use WOz methodology for testing robots. Ellen Francik, lead UX designer at Mayfield Robotics, needed to test how people reacted to the robot's responses to user input. Before the robot even had a microphone, she was able to test this scenario with a WOz setup.

The Wizard would use an iPad app, which was connected to the robot via Bluetooth, to control the robot's movements, sounds, and animations. When the user said a command to the robot or asked a question, the Wizard would play the appropriate sound and move the robot. In this way, Francik could test whether users understood the robot's (non-verbal) responses. Did the user know when the robot "said" yes? Could the user tell when it indicated a "got it!" response?

Because they were testing in the environment in which the robot would actually be used—in people's homes—they did not try to hide the Wizard. Francik said this was not an impediment; people were still game to interact with the robot, and the sessions proved highly valuable.

Conclusion

User testing VUI devices has many things in common with any kind of user testing: test through as many stages of development as possible; carefully choose your demographics; design your tasks to exercise the right features; don't lead the subject; and ask the right questions.

It can be more difficult to test VUI apps because traditional methods (user talking out loud as they test, screen capture software to record their actions) are often not appropriate. However, there are workarounds, such as testing before speech recognition has been implemented and having a Wizard play prompts, or doing a text-only version. Remember that it's important to test whether users can complete tasks in a satisfactory way, not just whether a cool feature works. Just because you *can* say "book me a taxi and then make a reservation and then send my mom flowers" doesn't mean any users actually *will* say it.

Data collection, as mention in Chapter 5, is an essential part of building a successful VUI. Collecting data during the testing phases is a great way to enhance your VUI early on. Learn how users talk and interact with your system via testing, and build your VUI accordingly.

[7]

Your Voice User Interface Is Finished! Now What?

You've done it! You've designed and developed your voice user interface (VUI)!

Now what?

It would be wonderful to be able to stop there, put your app out into the wild, and reap the benefits and rewards. But it's more complicated than that. For one thing, you need to ensure that everything has been thoroughly tested. Then, after you've launched, you need to actually verify whether your system is working. Fortunately, there are standardized methods for tracking and analyzing your system's performance, and you can use that information to tune and improve your VUI.

This chapter describes some VUI-specific testing activities, gets into detail about what needs to be logged, and provides instructions on what to do with all that data.

Prerelease Testing

First, let's get into testing. Presumably your app has by this point gone through some regular testing methods, making sure it works on different devices; you have run usability tests, and completed basic QA. Now let's talk about VUI-specific testing.

DIALOG TRAVERSAL TESTING

One type of testing that's crucial for VUIs is something that the interactive voice response (IVR) system world calls *Dialog Traversal Testing* (DTT). In this case, a "dialog" refers to a state in your conversational flow, usually one question followed by a user's response. It includes all transitions, error prompts, help prompts, or anything else that could happen at that state.

Here's a description from *Voice User Interface Design* of how it works for IVR systems:

> The purpose of Dialog Traversal Testing is to make sure that the system accurately implements the dialog specification in complete detail. You perform the test with the live system, over the telephone, exercising a test script that thoroughly traverses the dialog. The correct actions must be taken at each step, and the correct prompts must be played.
>
> Every dialog state must be visited during the test. Within each dialog state, every universal and every error condition must be tested. For example, you should try an out-of-grammar utterance to test the behavior in response to a recognition reject. You should try silence to test no-speech timeouts. You should impose multiple successive errors within dialog states to ensure proper behavior.[1]

Today's VUIs have much in common with the earlier IVR systems, but there are some differences. For example, you won't be calling your VUI over the phone—most likely, you're *using* the app *on* your phone. In addition, for something like a virtual assistant, the tree might be very wide, but very shallow. For example, the main prompt might be something to the effect of "How may I help you?" In this case, you need to test that all the basic functions can be correctly accessed from this point. The DTT does *not* test every possible way you might say each function, just that the functions can be reached. For more complex systems, complete DTT might be too expensive and difficult; if so, make sure to test as many best paths (and common error paths) as possible.

It's important to test errors here, as well: no-speech timeouts (when the user did not say anything), and no matches (something was recognized, but the system did not know what to do with it).

For VUIs that have a deeper, fixed, more conversational tree, visiting every state/dialog is essential. I often print out the flow diagram and jot down notes as I test (see Figure 7-1) Traversal testing is time

---

1   Cohen, M., Giangola, J., and Balogh, J. *Voice User Interface Design.* (Boston, MA: Addison-Wesley, 2004), 6, 8, 75, 218, 247-248, 250-251, 259.

consuming, and it will be tempting to skip states, but your users will thank you for your thoroughness. Or, at least they won't curse you for your mistakes.

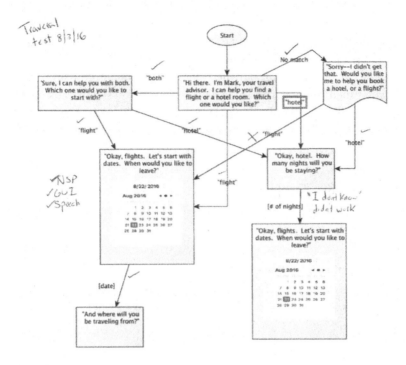

FIGURE 7-1.
Traversal testing flow example

RECOGNITION TESTING

In the IVR world, *recognition testing* is performed to ensure that the base recognition parameters are set correctly. It is generally done by a small set of people (10 to 20) who follow a predetermined script. (Figure 7-2 shows a sample script.)

In today's world of cloud-based speech recognition, there are fewer parameters to tune, but it can be a helpful exercise, nonetheless. As pointed out in *Voice User Interface Design*, one of the parameters to look out for here is the end-of-speech setting: saying phone numbers, for example, can require a longer-than-average end-of-speech timeout because people typically pause between sets. This parameter might be something you can set, depending on your speech recognition engine, and it's important to catch early on in your testing so your pilot users do not have to suffer.

It can also tease out common misrecognitions that you might need to add to your set of expected phrases. For example, a medical app I was designing commonly misrecognized "vial" as "vile" or even "file." Adding those up front meant more users would have success right out of the gate. As Anne Thyme-Gobbel points out, even using "medically tuned" dictionaries won't always solve this issue, because users are generally people who don't have a medical background, and they're using a few specific terms for their situation; this is a very different use case than, say, dictating medical notes.

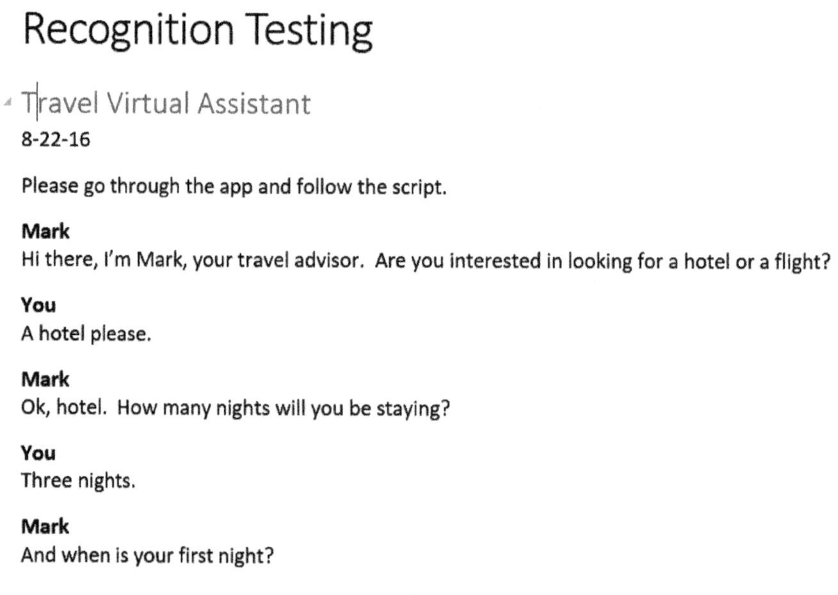

Recognition Testing

◢ Travel Virtual Assistant

8-22-16

Please go through the app and follow the script.

Mark
Hi there, I'm Mark, your travel advisor. Are you interested in looking for a hotel or a flight?

You
A hotel please.

Mark
Ok, hotel. How many nights will you be staying?

You
Three nights.

Mark
And when is your first night?

FIGURE 7-2.
Sample recognition testing script

LOAD TESTING

Load testing, or verifying that the system will perform under the stress of many concurrent user sessions, might be applicable, depending on what type of recognizer infrastructure you're using. Third-party services exist to help you simulate load tests for your mobile apps, which is a lot more sophisticated than the method we sometimes used in the early startup days at Nuance: namely, my coworker Madhavan running down the hall yelling "LOAD TEST!" so we'd all pick up our phones at the same time to call the system.

Load testing will inform you as to whether your backend will crash or slow down to a crawl when you hit a certain number of users, and it's much better to find that out during testing than when your app goes live!

Now that you've completed the testing phase, it's time to think about the launch of the first pilot.

Measuring Performance

Before starting your pilot, you need to define your goals. This will help determine what exactly you need to measure and, therefore, what the system needs to log. You should define your goals as early as possible so as to not be caught short right before launch when you discover your app doesn't track a crucial detail that your VP wants to see.

In *How to Build a Speech Recognition Application*, Bruce Balentine and David Morgan describe this process:

> Well before application launch, both the developer and the client for whom the application is being developed (marketing, sales, support, and other stakeholders) must state the goals and objectives of the application. For each objective, they must also characterize success or failure. Too often success is measured solely in terms of recognition accuracy. This is perhaps the worst metric. Is an application that obtains 90 precent accuracy and automates 85 percent of calls for a business better or worse than one that achieves 97 percent recognition and automates 40 percent of calls?[2]

As Balentine and Morgan state, it is crucial to involve stakeholders when defining these goals. Designers, marketing, sales, and other departments do not always share the same view on what needs to be measured. As a designer, you might be most interested in whether or not your users are able to utilize your system successfully and complete tasks. As the person in charge of business development, you might be

---

2   Balentine, B. and Morgan, D. *How to Build a Speech Recognition Application: A Style Guide for Telephony Dialogues.* (San Ramon, CA: EIG Press, 2001),213, 309–311.

most interested in how many transactions were automated. Business stakeholders do well involving their speech team in this process because they can help explain why something is difficult or easy to measure and why it might or might not actually measure what's desired.

If you work together to define these goals up front, you can determine what can and cannot be measured as well as lay out your criteria for success. Deciding on success criteria *after* the launch can lead to frustrations on both sides.

Here are some examples of success criteria:

- Sixty percent of users who start to make a hotel reservation complete it.

- Eighty-five percent of users complete a daily wellness check-in at least 20 days out of a month.

- The error rate for playing songs is less than 15 percent.

- Five hundred users download the app in the first month.

- The user satisfaction survey gives the app an average rating of at least four stars.

TASK COMPLETION RATES

One key measure of success for your VUI is *task completion rate*. Task completion is when the user has successfully started and completed one specific task. Balentine and Morgan refer to this as a "graceful conclusion."[3]

Your mobile app might have one task, or it might have many. Each of these tasks should be predefined in order to be measured. Determining when a task is complete sounds easy, but there are subtleties to keep in mind. Ann Thyme-Gobbel has an example from a credit card application. The "pay bill" task was considered successful if the user was able to pay his current balance. However, Thyme-Gobbel and her colleagues found a high percentage of users who dropped out before completing the task.

---

3 Balentine, B. and Morgan, D. *How to Build a Speech Recognition Application*, 213, 309–311.

At first, they were left scratching their heads as to why this was. Recognition performance was fine. Eventually they realized that many people quit after the *initial* part of the task: hearing their current balance and due date. After this discovery, the designers created two separate tasks—getting a balance and paying a bill—and the "pay bill" task did not *start* until the user went past the balance prompt and began the bill pay workflow.

As with the previous example, tasks can be considered complete before the end of the conversation. Another example of this is a healthcare app in which users can answer questions about their symptoms to determine if they should see a doctor. After an outcome is given, the user is offered the option to have information emailed to them. Is the task complete only if the user answers the question about email? It makes more sense to have a task labeled "Received health outcome," which is successful if the user reaches the outcome state, and then separately track how many people agree to receiving email.

Here are some examples of a successful task:

- User books a hotel room.
- User sets an alarm.
- User plays a song.
- User turns on the lights.
- User answers three questions in a trivia game.
- User takes her glucose measurement.
- User makes a payment to someone.
- User receives her estimated commute time.
- User searches for and finds a movie.

DROPOUT RATE

In addition to measuring whether users completed tasks, it is important to analyze *where* users drop out. If dropouts occur all along the workflow of a particular task, it can be difficult to ascertain why, but oftentimes there will be clusters of dropouts around particular states of the app. The following list outlines some common reasons for an earlier-than-expected dropout:

- User finished the task earlier than anticipated (such as the previous example of getting a bank balance)

- Prompt was confusing

- High rate of no-matches/out-of-grammars (e.g., user said something that was not expected in that state)

- User does not feel they're getting anywhere toward reaching their goal

When you locate a point in the process with a high dropout rate, it's important to examine the prompt(s) leading up to that state. It's always crucial to collect and transcribe what the user is saying. A common example is of a prompt that asks a question that *could* be answered with a "yes" or "no" but does not have the ability to handle that response, such as "Do you want to send the email, or cancel it?" One response to this sort of phrasing is "yes," but designers do not always build in a match for it, expecting instead to hear only variations of "send the email" or "cancel it."

It's also useful to see what the user did next. Did they leave the app entirely? Did they go back to the top? Did they try rephrasing the request or choosing a different category? If you have menus or categories, it might be that things are not grouped in a way that is clear to the user.

OTHER ITEMS TO TRACK

In addition to things such as task completion and dropout rates, there are other details that can be useful to record and analyze, such as where users are silent when they should speak, and where they most frequently interrupt the system.

Amount of time in the VUI

In the IVR days, a common measure was call duration. Generally, it was thought that a short time in the IVR system was preferable, because it indicated that the user was getting their task done quickly and efficiently.

Although you don't want your user wandering around your app in confusion or frustration, a longer duration is not always an indicator that things are not going well. Users can be highly tolerant of long interactions *if* they feel they are getting somewhere. Duration is not always tied to measuring user satisfaction or success. Thyme-Gobbel refers to this as "perceptual duration, rather than absolute duration," and says that "many things factor in to that, including quick response time, flatness of prompt delivery (monotone will seem longer), superfluous wording, lack of variation in responses, too many options (causes the user to think more), misrecognitions by the system... anything perceived of as annoying." In addition, users might be deliberately spending a long time in the app, such as listening to stock quotes over and over again. If the user feels in control, duration is not necessarily a bad thing.

Duration can be useful for other reasons, however. For example, if you are selling a daily conversation of some sort, such as an activity tracking VUI, business development stakeholders might be interested in the average length of the interaction. Users considering downloading the app might also be interested. It might be worth tracking for these types of reasons.

Barge-in

If you have barge-in enabled in your VUI, it is useful to track where users barge-in and whether it's too sensitive or not sensitive enough. Not all recognizers will allow you to tune barge-in parameters, but even if they do not, you can get insights into your app's performance by noting where users barge-in the most.

If your users barge-in frequently at particular or unexpected points, examine the prompt at which they barge-in as well as the prompt(s) leading up to it. Perhaps the prompt is too long. A crucial piece of this, however, is comparing barge-in rates with novice versus long-term usage. You might find a high barge-in rate in a particular place, but that only expert users barge-in. Rather than having the same set of prompts for both types of users, your VUI could have shortened prompts for users who have interacted more than a minimum number of times.

Speech versus GUI

Another interesting metric is looking at modality. Your mobile app might have many places in which users can touch the screen or speak. In certain cases, users might be more likely to use touch, whereas in others they prefer to use speech. This can help pinpoint where to invest resources; if there is a place in your app where users predominantly use touch, ensure that the GUI options are clear and accessible. If there is a point at which users almost always speak, you might want to minimize or remove GUI options (or only bring them in for backoff cases if speech is failing).

High no-speech timeouts, no matches

As mentioned previously, pay attention to states in which there is a high rate of no speech detected (NSP) timeouts or no matches (the user's words were correctly recognized, but the VUI does not have a programmed response to that utterance).

A high number of NSP timeouts can be an indication of a confusing prompt, or perhaps an indication that the user is being asked something they do not have handy, such as an account number. Examine the prompt, and if it is asking for a piece of information, provide a way for the user to pause or ask for help in order to find what's needed.

There are two types of no matches:

- Correct reject

- False reject

A *correct reject* means the user said something that was correctly not matched, because it was not an expected response for that state. For example, if the prompt asks, "What is your favorite color?" and the user responds, "I like to eat spaghetti," it's probably not something your VUI system will have a response for—nor should it, at least until we reach a level of AI and natural-language understanding seen in movies such as *Her*. These types of responses are called *out-of-domain*.

The other type of no match is a *false reject*, meaning that the user said something the VUI really *should* have been able to handle, but it did not. This often occurs in early stages of development, before a lot of user testing, because the designer has not anticipated the various ways users can phrase their requests. For example, a virtual assistant might have functionality to cancel appointments on a calendar, but not have anticipated a user saying, "I can't make it to my meeting on Thursday, so take it off my calendar," even though that is a perfectly legitimate request. These types of responses are called *in-domain*.

It is important to note that the distinction between in-domain and out-of-domain is purely academic. The recognizer rejects the utterance in both cases, and it is only after the utterances are transcribed and analyzed in the process of tuning that we can make the distinction between the two types of errors.

Another level of complexity includes responses that do answer the question, but require more intelligence on the part of the VUI. For example, in response to the question, "What is your favorite color?" a user could say, "The color of my house." One could imagine in the not-too-distant future handling responses such as these.

Finally, as mentioned in Chapter 5, there are the cases in which a failure occurred because the recognizer did not get it quite right—for example, the recognizer might misunderstand the user asking "What is the pool depth?" as "What is the pool death?" If this is a common occurrence, adding "pool death" to the accepted key phrases is straightforward, but won't always be anticipated during early design. In addition, using an *N*-best list would help with this issue; "pool depth" is a likely occurrence later in the list, and walking through it until a more relevant match occurs, rather than just choosing the first, will automatically improve your VUI's accuracy.

This example is another reminder that there are multiple failure points that can occur in a VUI: the automated speech recognition (ASR), the natural-language understanding (NLU), and accessing appropriate content from the backend. When one of these fails, it doesn't matter to the user which one it was, only that it failed. It's important to think about all of these pieces when designing your VUI.

Tracking points at which the user spoke but the wrong thing happened is crucial to the success of your VUI. Users will quickly lose trust in your system if there are too many failures with speech. If you track failure points and have a continuous plan to improve (by rewording prompts so users know what to say, fixing flow issues, and enhancing recognition performance by adding additional key phrases, and retraining your NLU models) your system can quickly improve and keep users coming back.

Navigation

If your app has a Previous or Back button, tracking usage can lead to important insights. Points at which there is frequent use of the Back button often indicate that the user was misled into thinking that was the correct place to go. One strategy to address this is to allow users to get to the same place from multiple starting locations.

Consider a tech support application that asks the user to choose between different help topics, such as "Internet" versus "email." Although your website FAQ might group questions underneath these as very different, in a user's mental model there can be a lot of crossover. For example, if the user states, "My email isn't working," this could very well be an issue with the user's WiFi, which is also under the "Internet" topic.

If you have a "repeat" function, examine where there is heavy usage of this. It might indicate that your prompt is too long, or too wordy, making it difficult for users to comprehend the first time. Keep in mind that many users find it more difficult to remember auditory information than visual. Consider breaking it down into multiple steps or adding more visual cues. In addition to the deliberate "repeat," it's a good idea to document repeated queries, as well. For example, if your user keeps asking the same thing, such as, "What is the weather this week?" it's good to dig into why.

Latency

Many recognition engines provide information about latency, meaning how long it takes the recognizer to trigger on end-of-speech detection and return a recognition result. If your latency is too high, users will not think that they've been heard and will repeat themselves, which can cause problems. The Google Cloud Speech API provides a Dashboard to show this information (Figure 7-3).

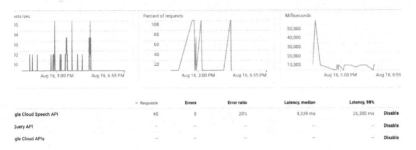

	Requests	Errors	Error ratio	Latency, median	Latency, 98%	
gle Cloud Speech API	40	8	20%	4,339 ms	25,200 ms	**Disable**
Juery API	-	-	-	-	-	**Disable**
gle Cloud APIs	-	-	-	-	-	**Disable**

FIGURE 7-3.
Google Speech Dashboard

Whole call recording

Although much of what will be analyzed is done on a per-utterance level (meaning one response, or turn, from the user, such as "red" or "I want to go to Golden Gate Park" or "Can you please find me a restaurant that's open tonight and is within a 10-minute drive?"), sometimes it can be useful to view interactions as part of a whole.

In the IVR world, this was referred to as *whole call recording*. Instead of just recording the utterances that are the user's responses, everything, including what the system says, is recorded as one long chunk. This requires a lot more room to store, of course, and is generally done only on a subset of calls.

A less memory-intensive method is to re-create the conversation by stitching together the system prompts that would have been played, with the utterances. If barge-in is enabled, you'll need the barge-in information, as well, to re-create when and where it occurred.

Listening to the whole call can reveal issues that you might not see when looking at one point in time. If your user is 10 turns into the conversation when things go wrong, listening to what happened up until that point can sometimes shed light.

However, you can also identify many dialog issues from re-created calls. In the early days of Nuance, one of the designers spent all his commute to and from work listening to recordings of calls to deployed systems: "As the traffic problems in Silicon Valley increased, our performance improved."[4]

Select calls randomly to get a good cross-section; you don't want only smooth calls or only calls with errors. Because the types of users can also vary based on the time of day and the day of week, don't be tempted to take a very short sampling for your calls; instead, try to sample over the course of a week at a minimum.

When re-creating conversations on a multimodal app, it will be necessary to show the screen interactions, as well.

This type of analysis might require some homegrown tools because there is not a lot on the market to do this. At Volio, we had a Conversation Dashboard (originally created by Volio's CTO, Bernt Habermeier). For each turn in the conversation, the dashboard showed what the system said, what the user said, and what happened next (Figure 7-4). It also had a video playback, so you could listen and watch the user's response.

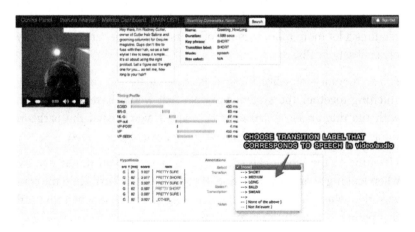

FIGURE 7-4.
Volio's Conversation Dashboard

---

4 Cohen, M., Giangola, J., and Balogh, J. *Voice User Interface Design.* (Boston, MA: Addison-Wesley, 2004), 6, 8, 75, 218, 247-248, 250-251, 259.

Logging

We've discussed many things that are important to measure, but to measure them, the information must first be logged. Without logging, when you launch your app into the wild, you will be blind. You will not know how well, or how poorly, your system is performing. Your users might be failing, but if you don't use proper logging, you will not know.

Talk to the development team at the beginning of any VUI project so that they understand the need to build logging in from the early stages. It is much more difficult to add logging information after launch. Information to log includes the following:

- Recognition result (what the recognizer heard when the user spoke, including confidence scores)

- N-best list, if available (list of possible hypotheses)

- Audio of user's utterance for each state, including pre- and post-endpointed utterances (for transcriptions, since the recognition result is not 100 percent accurate)

- If recognition did match to something, what it matched to

- Errors: no-speech timeouts (including timing information), no match, recognition errors

- State names (or other way to track where in the app the user traversed)

- Latency

- Barge-in information, if barge-in is enabled

It is important to log utterances and audio even when speech *failed*, including if the user says more than one thing in a given state. Imagine a virtual travel assistant that is asking the user for her departure airport. The screen shows a list of airports in Washington that the user can either tap or say. Here is a sequence:

1. User says, "Pasco, Washington."

2. Although Pasco is a valid airport, user was misrecognized as "Pass co airport."

3. Nothing happens (because this is a multimodal state, there is no "I'm sorry" error prompt).

4. User repeats, "I said Pasco, Washington!" but is again misrecognized as "Pats go airport."

5. Nothing happens.

6. User is frustrated, taps Pasco, instead.

Some developers might log only the final result that created the next action, but in doing so, important information is lost. Knowing where and how the user failed is key to improving the system.

It's best to log information after each turn in the conversation because the user might quit the app abruptly, or the app might crash. If you're only logging best-case scenario, when the user comes to a graceful conclusion, you will be missing important pieces of data.

It should go without saying that the audio information recorded should be anonymized and not used for things outside of analysis.

Transcription

Before you can accurately analyze system performance, one more key task is necessary: having humans listen to and transcribe (by hand) the utterances of users speaking to the VUI.

"But wait," you're saying. "I heard speech recognition is 92 percent accurate these days! I'll just use it to autotranscribe everything. Much cheaper."

It's true that, in many cases, speech recognition results are highly accurate. However, in many cases, they are not. And in this case, you're using what the users actually said to build and improve your dataset. Building a dataset with faulty data is not a recipe for success. As Balentine and Morgan say, "The only accurate way to determine speech recognition performance is by logging each individual utterance and then transcribing it offline.[5]

---

5   Balentine, B. and Morgan, D. *How to Build a Speech Recognition Application*, 213, 309–311.

Transcription does cost money, but you cannot build a good VUI without transcribing at least some of your data. There are companies out there that are dedicated to transcribing, such as Appen, which is a veteran in the field, but there are many other smaller companies that offer the service, as well. QA companies can sometimes do this, too, if provided with the right tools. Planning ahead again comes in handy here because your audio must be in certain formats for the company you choose.

At Volio, part of the Conversation Dashboard tool included a place to write down the transcription. Our QA team would play back the user's response in the video window, and write down exactly what the user said (see Figure 7-5).

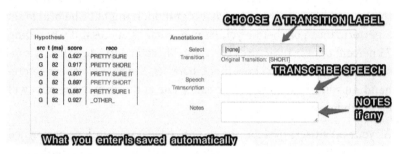

FIGURE 7-5.
Volio's transcription tool

Armed with the speech recognition results, matches, and audio transcriptions, you have what you need to analyze performance and see how your VUI is really doing.

Release Phases

As with any new technology released to the wild, it's best to roll it out in phases, rather than release it to the entire world at once.

PILOT

If possible, begin with a pilot. Pilots can range from just a few users to a few hundred. This type of rollout is important so that you can identify any show-stopper bugs at the outset. Pilots are also valuable for VUIs because as much QA testing and user testing as you can do up front still won't prepare you for all the ways in which users talk to your system:

> There is no way to evaluate the great variety of ways people will talk to the system until you collect data from users engaged in real, task-oriented behavior, **performing tasks that matter to them**. [Emphasis mine][6]

If you are able to, plan on several (short) pilots; this way, you can quickly roll out and test improvements to recognition. It might be helpful to set a performance goal before you launch, such as successfully handling 75 percent of user utterances correctly. This starting rate will vary considerably depending on how much data you are able to collect beforehand. In some cases, the performance rate at the start of the pilot will be much lower.

As your pilot users exercise the system, have transcriptions performed on a daily basis, and analyze each utterance. When you identify false rejects, or false accepts, update your key phrases/models and push them out.

Surveys

Another useful way to get feedback is of course to run a survey. Although it's common to run surveys via a third-party website such as SurveyMonkey, you can also let your VUI give the survey. Users are more likely to do a survey when it's within the app, rather than having to click a link at a later time. Figure 7-6 shows a sample survey with the Sensely avatar asking the questions. Users can speak or use touch.

Keep the survey a reasonable length (generally no more than five questions), and allow for an "Anything else?" open-ended response.

---

6   Cohen, M., Giangola, J., and Balogh, J. *Voice User Interface Design*. (Boston, MA: Addison-Wesley, 2004), 6, 8, 75, 218, 247-248, 250-251, 259.

FIGURE 7-6.
Survey conducted via avatar

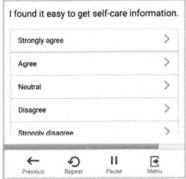

Thyme-Gobbel suggests using a different persona or avatar to ask the survey questions, not the one who performed the task. For example, if a male avatar helped the user schedule an appointment, a female avatar could ask if the user enjoyed using the app.

In addition, if you ask a quick yes/no question after the task was completed, such as, "Was I able to answer your question?" it can give you a head start in looking into potential problems without combing through the logs.

Finally, it's important to remember that surveys are inherently biased: generally speaking, those who choose to take a survey are the ones who are the most or the least satisfied. Keeping your survey short can increase engagement; a simple yes/no or rating might be sufficient.

Analysis

You've logged everything you need, run your pilot, and transcribed your utterances. What to do with all this data?

First, examine your in-grammar and out-of-grammar rates. These terms are more germane to the IVR world, but the concepts still apply for VUIs. Here are definitions from *Voice User Interface Design* (examples mine, in response to the question, "What's your favorite color?")

In-grammar data

- *Correct accept:* The recognizer returned the correct answer. ["My favorite color is red." → "red"]

- *False accept:* The recognizer returned an incorrect answer. ["I blew past that question but my favorite's teal"] → "blue"]

- *False reject:* The recognizer could not find a good match to any path in the grammar and therefore rejected rather returned an answer. ["I think magenta is nice." → no match]

Out-of-grammar data

- *Correct reject:* The recognizer correctly rejected the input. ["I think I would like to book a hotel" → no match]

- *False accept:* The recognizer returned an answer that is, by definition, wrong because the input was not in the grammar. ["I read the paper" → "red"]

Although these categories are important for analysis, it's not something the user needs to know about:

> From the point of view of the callers, the distinction between in-grammar and out-of-grammar is irrelevant. All they know is that they said something, and the dialog with the system is not proceeding as they expect.[7]

Most modern mobile apps are not dealing with grammars per se, but the general concepts are still a useful way to think about your system performance. In-grammar refers to things the user said that *should* be recognized; they are in-domain for that particular place in the workflow. Out-of-grammar means that the user said something that you have (deliberately) left out.

---

7   Cohen, M., Giangola, J., and Balogh, J. *Voice User Interface Design.* (Boston, MA: Addison-Wesley, 2004), 6, 8, 75, 218, 247-248, 250-251, 259.

It's important to maintain a balance between accepts and rejects. If you overgeneralize and try to accept as many things as possible, you end up with cases in which your user clearly did not say the right thing, but you recognized *something* anyway. If you don't make it robust enough, however, you won't have to worry about recognizing things you shouldn't, but you won't recognize enough things that you should.

Other parameters and design elements can be adjusted, as well. Let's take a look at them.

CONFIDENCE THRESHOLDS

Most ASR systems return a confidence score along with their result. As discussed in Chapter 2, you can use confidence scores to determine confirmation strategies. For example, results above a certain threshold can be implicitly confirmed ("OK, San Francisco.") and in the middle threshold can be explicitly confirmed ("Sounds like you said San Francisco. Is that right?")

If you're using confidence scores to determine your confirmation strategy, it's important to verify that it's set correctly at each state. You might find that different states need different confidence thresholds. Ideally, you'll want to play with the thresholds and rerun your data to optimize the values.

END-OF-SPEECH TIMEOUTS

Different states in your app might require different values of the end of speech. If you can customize these, examine your data to see if people are frequently cut off. A common example, as mentioned previously, is reading groupings of numbers, such as phone numbers or credit cards. For some recognizer engines, you can configure a different value of end of speech timeout for finals versus nonfinals in the grammar, allowing users to pause between groups of digits in a credit card number, yet being snappy at detecting the end-of-speech when the complete card number has been spoken. Another case is when an open question such as "How are you doing?" or "Tell me more about that" is presented to the user; oftentimes, people will pause while telling the VUI the information. You need to strike a balance between not cutting people off and not waiting too long to detect end of speech—waiting too long can cause people to think they were not heard.

INTERIM RESULTS VERSUS FINAL RESULTS

Some ASR tools, including Google's, allow you to receive real-time *interim results*. This means that as several words are recognized, your app can see the results. Your VUI can match on the user input before the user has even finished speaking. This can make the app very snappy, but it has drawbacks, as well. For example, if you're working on a pizza-ordering app and you say "What toppings would you like?" your user might reply, "Pepperoni, olives, mushrooms."

If you're matching on interim results, you might see that "pepperoni" has matched to one of the ingredients, and finish the turn. This will serve to cut the user off before he has finished speaking, and you will miss some of the ingredients, too.

Look at the data to determine if matching on interim results will be appropriate. For simple yes/no states, it can be a great idea.

CUSTOM DICTIONARIES

Your VUI might have certain brand names or unusual terms that are rarely (or not at all) recognized. Many ASR tools offer the opportunity to customize the vocabulary, putting specified items as higher probabilities.

Nuance, for example, has a "My Vocabulary" section, in which you can add your own words (Figure 7-7). One example from its Vocabulary Guide is "Eminem": if you're creating a music app, you'll want "Eminem" to have a higher probability of being recognized than "M&M."

Another example, mentioned previously in this chapter, is a medical app in which patients ask about "vials" of medication. Adding "vial" to your vocabulary will give that a higher probability than "vile," which is what the speech recognition engine might be more likely to return.

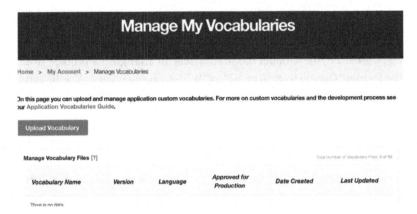

FIGURE 7-7.
Nuance's custom vocabulary tool

Google's Speech API provides "word and phrase hints" for this task. This allows you to boost the probability of certain words, or add new words such as proper names or domain-specific vocabulary.

PROMPTS

In addition to looking at parameters, it's important to examine your prompts, as well. Subtle changes in wording can often affect how users speak:

> For example, if the prompt says "Where are you going?" callers are more likely to give an answer such as "I am going to San Francisco," whereas if the prompt says "What's the destination city?" an answer such as, "My destination city is San Francisco" is more likely.[8]

If you notice a lot of no matches, be sure to look at your prompt wording. Are you asking the question in such a way to get the type of answers you're expecting? In addition, don't just lump similar types

---

8   Cohen, M., Giangola, J., and Balogh, J. *Voice User Interface Design*. (Boston, MA: Addison-Wesley, 2004), 6, 8, 75, 218, 247-248, 250-251, 259.

of responses. For example, even basic yes/no key phrases might not always be the same. Look at the difference between these two yes/no questions:

- "Are you finished?" might generate "Yes I am"
- "Is that correct?" might generate "Yes it is"

Even something as simple as word ordering can modify user's responses. Thyme-Gobbel has an example of changing a prompt from the format "Do you want A or B?" to "Which do you want—A or B?" and greatly increasing correct responses.

Tools

At this time, not many tools exist to easily allow designers to improve their VUIs based on user data. It might be necessary to build your own.

One thing that is essential is an easy and robust way to enhance your key phrases. As you analyze the transcriptions and no matches, it will quickly become clear where you need to add or enhance your expected recognition phrases. For example, perhaps you are a US designer designing for a UK dialing app, and you discover that a lot of users in the UK say "ring" for making a call. You want a tool that will easily allow you to add this phrase and push out the change without having to access a database, or roll out a new version of the app.

At Volio, we had a tool with which we could easily see, for a particular state, where "no matches" had occurred. It provided a drag-and-drop method for adding key phrases, and a simple way to push these changes into the testing environment (Figure 7-8).

You might have multiple users of your dashboard. External users might want to see details at a higher level. The Sensely Conversation Dashboard shows what the avatar says, what the user said (the recognition result), and any information collected from devices (Figure 7-9).

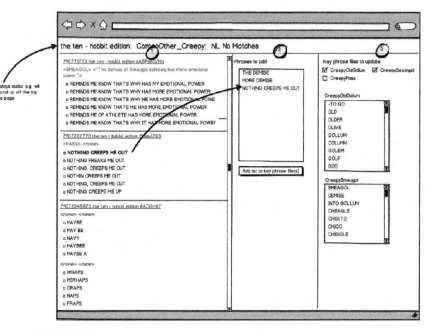

FIGURE 7-8.
Mock-up of Volio's tool to add new key phrases.

09/16/16 09:11 AM ▼

1. *Good morning. Its time for your daily check in. How are you doing?*

   Good

2. *Thanks for sharing with me. Lets get started. When you have your scale ready, press Continue. Tap the scale with your foot until you see the zero point zero. I will wait for it to connect. We're all set. Please step on the scale.*

   264.9 pounds

FIGURE 7-9.
The Sensely Conversation Dashboard

Voxcom, which develops speech recognition apps for call centers, has an automated script that generates system reports automatically from its call logs (Figure 7-10). It's very useful for immediately determining key factors such as dropout rates (how far do users get), and how frequently users had to correct responses.

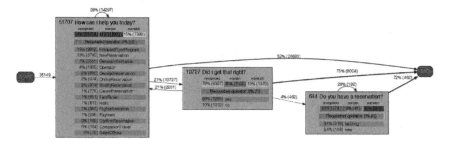

FIGURE 7-10.
Voxcom's automated graph, for an airline call steering app (courtesy Vitaly Yurchenko)

REGRESSION TESTING

When you've analyzed your data, reworked problem prompts, and tweaked your parameters, it's important to determine if it actually improved performance.

Don't just assume. Instead, take your data (audio recordings), and rerun them through the newly tuned system. Do your no match rates drop? Does your false accept rate improve?

Regression testing provides a robust way to ensure that your improvements work well and do not break anything. It's possible to fix one problem while unintentionally causing another; regression testing will show these issues *before* you go live with updates.

Conclusion

Launching your app is an exciting milestone. Because VUIs include a complex input method—speech—it's particularly difficult to be sure that it will perform exactly as expected.

Luckily, there are ways to monitor how your app is doing and allow the designer to quickly improve performance. It's crucial to log all the information that might be needed, so that analysis can proceed as soon

as you begin collecting data. Transcription, in which humans transcribe what users actually said, is essential to understand how your
system is truly performing.

Define success measures and task completion definitions at the outset,
during the design phase, so that there is agreement among stakeholders,
and developers have time to build infrastructure for all the logging tasks.

Tracking your speech failure points and having a way to quickly make
improvements is essential for successful VUIs.

[8]

Voice-Enabled Devices and Cars

THIS CHAPTER DISCUSSES REAL-WORLD examples of VUIs outside of the mobile app world. This includes devices such as home assistants like the Amazon Echo, and smartwatches. It also includes voice systems in the car. Some examples are of real-world, existing technology, whereas others are for things on the near horizon.

It's the beginning of the evolution of these devices, and the landscape will be changing rapidly, but this is an introduction of what is to come. I owe a great deal of thanks to other experts in these areas who contributed to this chapter.

Devices

There are a variety of voice-enabled devices in the market today. Home assistants such as the Amazon Echo and Google Home allow you to control the lights, set timers, listen to music, and perform many other tasks. Watches and other wearables help you track your fitness and leave your phone in your purse or pocket. Some televisions also provide voice-assisted remote controls.

HOME ASSISTANTS

One of the most common voice-enabled devices are the home assistants. Amazon Echo is currently leading the market, and Google Home was just released. Other devices are on the horizon, such as Athom's Homey, Mycroft, Ivee, and Jibo.

The Amazon Echo is a black cylinder, about nine inches tall, with a light ring at the top edge (Figure 8-1). Its primary interface is via voice with Amazon's Alexa Voice Service, but it has a companion mobile app for setting up your account, adding "Skills" (features), and showing you what's been recognized. The ring on top can be physically rotated to adjust the volume, or you can ask Alexa to do that for you. It has an array of seven microphones under the light ring, to allow for far-field voice recognition. To ask the Echo a question, or issue a command, you must preface it with the wake word "Alexa."

The Echo is constantly listening for its wake word. It does this processing locally; this means that what it hears when you haven't said the wake word is not stored. When it hears someone say "Alexa," the ring at the top lights up in blue, and it listens for a few seconds for your query. Here are some examples of things that you can say:

- "Alexa, set a timer for 10 minutes."

- "Alexa, play 'Call and Answer' by the Barenaked Ladies."

- "Alexa, who is the president of the United States?"

- "Alexa, what's my commute?" [You can set your location via the mobile app.]

- "Alexa, add milk to my shopping list."

It currently retails for $180. Amazon sells two other (cheaper) models as well: the Tap and the Dot. The Tap (Figure 8-2) requires users to physically tap the device before it will begin listening; the Dot is a squatter version of the Echo, with lower-quality speakers.

FIGURE 8-1.
The Amazon Echo

FIGURE 8-2.

The Amazon Tap

Alexa has a sense of humor, as well. If you ask Alexa, "Are you Skynet?" she'll say "I had nothing to do with Skynet. Don't worry."

In addition, Amazon has opened its doors to allow developers to add their own "Skills," of which there are more than a thousand, such as playing *Jeopardy!*, getting a compliment, or asking for advice on a child's illness.

At its 2016 I/O conference, Google announced its own home assistant, Google Home (Figure 8-3). As described on its blog:

> Google Home is a voice-activated product that brings the Google assistant to any room in your house. It lets you enjoy entertainment, manage everyday tasks, and get answers from Google—all using conversational speech. With a simple voice command, you can ask Google Home to play a song, set a timer for the oven, check your flight, or turn on your lights. It's designed to fit your home with customizable bases in different colors and materials. Google Home will be released later this year.

FIGURE 8-3.
Google Home

Homey (Figure 8-4) is made by Athom, a Netherlands-based company. It will hook up to other devices in your home, such as a smart oven, television, or light switch.

Homey uses the wake word, "Hey, Homey," to start listening. One interesting feature of Homey (based on its demo video) is that it can ask relevant follow-up questions, such as when someone asks to watch a TV program: "Hey, Homey, I'd like to watch *Star Trek*," Homey follows up with "Would you like subtitles with that?" Ideally, Homey would know if the user commonly wanted subtitles, and not ask every single time. The demo video also shows Homey dimming the lights and turning on the television.

Mycroft is unusual in that it has a male persona. Unlike the Echo, it has a "face"—an animated screen that allows Mycroft to show expressions, as shown in Figure 8-5. An open source device, it is due to ship in 2017.

FIGURE 8-4.
Athom's Homey

FIGURE 8-5.
Mycroft

Figure 8-6 shows Jibo, which is even more animated—in addition to its "face" (which also has a screen), it can swivel around. For example, if Jibo is facing away from you, and you say, "Hey, Jibo," Jibo will turn toward you. Jibo is due to ship in the United States and Canada in 2017.

FIGURE 8-6.
Jibo

When you ask Jibo "What's your favorite movie?", it plays the opening music from *Star Wars*, and spins around while showing a TIE fighter flying. At the moment, Jibo appears to be the device most capable of showing lots of personality.

Personality is an important consideration for your device. If you imbue your device with a warm, cute personality, that might be very appropriate for day-to-day family interactions, but will people trust it to deliver medical advice? Personality is more than just the voice you choose and inserting cute responses; understanding the context in which the VUI is being used and the user's expectations and mood is also a key component.

Reasons for the success of these devices include superior microphone design as well as advances in signal capture and signal enhancing software. The Amazon Echo reliably understands requests from across the room. It's great for hands-free tasks when you're in the kitchen. If you try "Hey, Siri" or "Ok Google" from across the room, you're unlikely to get a response (although I sometimes see them accidentally summoned during meetings!) This is partially by design; your phone is generally meant to be used when close to you, whereas the Echo is designed for use in a larger space. However, it also has to do with the microphone technology.

Although you can do many things a home assistant can offer by using your mobile phone, the frictionless nature of the hands-free home-assistant device means users are much more likely to use voice. It might seem minor—how much trouble is it to pick up a phone, unlock it, say "Ok Google," and make a request?—but it actually makes a big difference in usage. In addition, many people are accustomed to using their phones primarily by typing and haven't necessarily made the switch to interacting by voice.

Of course, the lack of a screen also affects user experience. When a device does not understand a command, you need to be sure to let your user know. As discussed in Chapter 2, the Amazon Echo has different methods for handling errors: in some cases, the light simply fades, signifying it *really* didn't understand you. In other cases, it knows you asked a question, so Alexa will say, "I'm sorry, I didn't understand the question I heard." It also provides context-sensitive help in some instances; for example, if you request a volume level that's not between 1 and 10, Alexa will remind you of the range.

Other things to consider with a home-assistant device are whether it will differentiate between people in a household with more than one user. Will anyone be allowed to use the device, or will it be "locked down" to certain users? This might not matter in terms of who's asking it to play a song, but letting anyone ask for the current bank balance, order hundreds of dollars of products (helloooo, gummy worms!) or to unlock the door, is not wise.

Designing for Devices Without Screens

In the following discussion, Ian Menzies, senior voice UX designer at Lab126 (Amazon), talks about some of the best practices for designing for VUIs with no visual feedback.

Many of the challenges facing VUI design for screen-free devices are similar to those faced by VUI design for IVR systems in the past. Here are some best practices:

Keep it short

Speech is ephemeral, transitory, and linear, so messaging needs to be crisp and clear to minimize cognitive load and avoid friction. Long or complex sentences, corporate or technical jargon, or an over-abundance of options will get in the way of quick and easy understanding. Less is definitely more.

Keep it natural

Customers should not have to learn how to speak to a VUI. It's the job of the designer and the technology to make sure the interface is as natural and human as possible.

Providing feedback

If a screen is available, recognition results can be shown in text, but with a speech-only system, feedback is limited to the same constrained audio channel that's used for other input and output. It's important to let the customer know what we understood, but to do so in a crisp, natural, and conversational manner.

Design for ambiguity

There's often possible ambiguity built into a speech interaction, and a VUI needs to plan for that. Siri can simply ask, "Which one?" and pop a list of options on the screen, but that's not possible with a speech-only system. If there are only a few options to choose from, it's usually possible to design natural-sounding disambiguation, but that becomes more challenging as the number of options grows.

Support corrections

Mistakes happen, and although its often not difficult for a customer to simply start over, having to start over is not a good user experience. With a screen, corrections can be provided manually, but a VUI should support the same kind of correction people use in speech all the time, often without giving it any thought. One-step correction is a common technique used for corrections, where a customer can reject a faulty recognition and provide a correction in a single turn. For example, if the system asks "That was Boston, right?", the user could respond with "No, Austin." Implementing one-step correction is often a challenge for the technology, but a great customer experience when it works.

Timing is important

Unlike a GUI, where a question can stay on the screen for a minute or an hour without fading, a VUI needs to respect generally employed timing rules from human dialog. In conversation between people, pauses between speakers are usually less than 400 milliseconds, and long silences can be disruptive, so VUIs need to employ timing strategies that are appropriate for people, not those that are possible for the technology.

Lists are hard

Screens and text are great for consuming lists or presenting lots of structured data. Consider a menu, a Contacts list, or credit card statement—all are easy to browse visually, but would be painful to review in a VUI. If structured data needs to be presented in a VUI, it's important to consider the amount of data delivered in a single turn, the speed of delivery, and the pauses between items. Is the list primarily for review, or can the customer edit the content? Is the customer somewhat familiar with the content, or not at all familiar? Could a question or two reduce the list from many items to just a few? User testing is always a good investment when implementing a list in a VUI.

Text-to-speech has limitations

The quality of text-to-speech, or TTS, has improved a lot in recent years, but compared to natural human speech or text on a screen, it still has limitations. In natural speech, pauses as well as variations in tempo, stress, and intonation can be used to highlight or emphasize segments of speech. On a screen, text can be highlighted, underlined, italicized, or set in a different color or font to show emphasis. Applying variations in prosody for TTS is more challenging. Speech Synthesis Markup Language, or SSML, provides some tools for modifying pitch, speed, volume, and contour in TTS, but adds complexity to highly dynamic TTS. TTS is great for a wide variety of skills and features, but stand-up comics don't have anything to worry about in the near future.

Shamitha Somashekar, a principal product manager at Amazon Lab126 who has worked on the Echo since the early days, agrees with Menzies that many of the design principles from interactive voice response (IVR) systems are still very relevant. The Amazon Echo is not an IVR system, but basic computer–human interface principles still apply.

Somashekar says one of the challenges of working on the Echo is the huge amount of data they receive. Transcribing data is an important part of understanding and improving VUI system performance, but she says there is simply too much to describe by humans, so they must come up with other ways to look at the data.

Another challenge they are highly focused on is discoverability—how to teach people what they can do with the Echo. Most users don't want to be told to look at their phone; they want to do everything through the Echo itself.

According to Somashekar, the Echo's "Simon Says" skill is a big hit among users (especially when they also have an Echo remote and can stand in the other room). Say, "Alexa, Simon Says X" and it will repeat what it heard. She says it's used by parents to get their kids to go to bed—when Alexa says, "Jack, time to brush your teeth," kids listen.

Somashekar also points out that attenuation is a well-liked feature of the Echo. If you say, "Alexa," while music is playing on your Echo, the music doesn't stop, but the volume is lowered so that you can still hear Alexa speak. If you're listening to a book, however, it's paused. This might seem like a small difference, but it translates to a much nicer user experience.

Somashekar says the light ring on the Echo is an important design factor because it builds trust with the user. Users know the Echo is only sending speech to the cloud when the light ring is on, and for something that is "always on," trust is a huge issue.

For more great tips and real-world examples, check out the Alexa Skills Kit Voice Design Best Practices at *http://amzn.to/2fPPJXf/*.

WATCHES/BANDS/EARBUDS

Another type of device that is slowly gaining popularity is the smartwatch. Some smartwatches are sleek and elegant and look like regular watches (Figure 8-7); others are much more obviously a "gadget." The watch is paired with your phone, so you can have access to the calendar, answer phone calls, and see text messages. Microsoft offers a bracelet device, as well (Figure 8-8).

FIGURE 8-7.
Apple Watch, Moto 360, Pebble

FIGURE 8-8.
Microsoft Band

Smartwatches promise users a more streamlined life, because those users won't need to keep checking their phone for updates. (Instead, they might constantly glance at their wrists, making you think they're checking the time and are in a rush to be somewhere.) Most smart-watches are programmable, so you can choose to display only the updates that interest you.

The Moto 360 can respond to commands in a similar way as your Android phone: simply say, "Ok Google," to have it start listening, and then ask, for example, "When's my next haircut?", order a ride from Lyft, or reply to a chat message.

Although smartwatches have been around for a few years, their expense (and size) are a barrier. More manufacturers are beginning to think about designing for women's smaller wrist sizes.

There are also design challenges: no one wants to type a message on their watch, so a good VUI is key. There is some screen real estate, but only a certain amount of information can be displayed.

Finally, not everyone is comfortable with speaking in public to their watch, Dick Tracy–style.

Another new development are wireless earbuds, such as Apple's AirPods. These are like earbuds without the wires that have a direct Bluetooth connection to your phone—and to Siri. By double-tapping, you can speak to Siri, and she'll speak back in your ears. Airpods use beamforming microphones to filter out external noise and focus on the sounds of your voice.

Although not a watch or a bracelet, there's another wearable device that bears mentioning: ThinkGeek's *Star Trek* ComBadge, shown in Figure 8-9.

FIGURE 8-9.
The *Star Trek* "Com Badge" from ThinkGeek

When connected to your mobile phone via Bluetooth, this badge will allow you to answer phone calls and issue commands. It's due out in 2017. In many people's minds, the *Star Trek* ComBadge is the canonical example of a VUI: the ability to issue voice commands from anywhere, merely by tapping or speaking the wake word, and have a powerful computer reply. We're inching ever closer to the imagined future.

OTHER DEVICES

Television providers have also invested heavily in VUI. As one example, Comcast has a voice-enabled remote control called the X1 Voice Remote with which users can control their television. It requires users to press (and hold) a button on the remote itself and then speak a command. When the button is pressed, the television screen displays a blue bar at the bottom with the text "listening." Commands include saying a channel name, such as CNN; when the remote has recognized the channel, it's displayed in the bottom bar, which quickly disappears when the channel has been changed.

Other commands include:

- "Watch NBC"
- "Find kids movies"
- "Launch Sports app"
- "Show me what's on tonight at seven"
- "Turn on closed captioning"
- "Show me settings"
- "Show me movies with Harrison Ford"

Requiring users to hold down a button on the remote, rather than use a wake word, works for this model. When you're watching TV, you're likely to be stationary and have the remote nearby. It also increases the recognition performance.

Neither the remote nor the TV speak back to the user; instead, visual feedback is used on the television to confirm the command.

Cars and Autonomous Vehicles

Speech recognition was first introduced in cars in the mid-2000s. In 2005, IBM partnered with Honda to add in-car navigation features and even listen to Zagat restaurant reviews. In 2007, Ford utilized speech recognition technology from Microsoft/Tellme and created SYNC, which used Bluetooth to connect to mobile phones and allowed drivers to make voice-dialed phone calls. Later versions of SYNC enabled users the ability to play music and get traffic information, among other features.

CHALLENGES OF DESIGNING VUI FOR THE CAR

Designing VUIs for cars has many challenges. First, there's the noise factor: driving along at 70 MPH, music blaring, passengers talking, does not make for an easy recognition task. Even with no music playing or people talking, road noise alone makes it difficult. Finding the right placement for the microphone is also a tough design job.

In addition, cars have a slower upgrade cycle than mobile phones or other devices connected to the Internet. Upgrading the speech software in the car, until recently, required the owner to bring the car back to the dealer. Making improvements was much more difficult.

Although some of these things are changing (such as a Tesla being able to automatically upgrade its software), VUIs in the car are often frustrating and difficult to use. In the J.D. Power 2015 Initial Quality Study of top reported problems in the car (with #10 being cup holders, #2 being Bluetooth pairing and connectivity), the number one problem was voice-recognition systems. From the report:

> Built-in voice-recognition systems that frequently don't recognize and/or misinterpret commands continues to be the most troublesome area in the new-vehicle ownership experience. The complaint rate is the highest in the study—nearly triple that for problems related to interior materials that scuff and/or soil easily and excessive wind noise.

This is assuming that you can get your phone to pair to the car via Bluetooth, the second biggest complaint in the list. This pairing process can be painful and time consuming, especially if you are in a household with more than one driver/mobile device.

Even the simplest aspect, push-to-talk to enable the car to begin listening, lacks design consistency when it comes to how many controls or where controls are placed. In a recent video instructing people on how to use the voice commands in their 2016 Honda Odyssey, the video actually calls this out, saying, "Make sure you press the *talk* button when you want to use voice commands, not the phone pickup button." I've experienced this confusion myself in my car, pressing the off-hook (what the heck does off-hook even mean in a car?) when the talk button was required.

DESIGNING FOR IN THE CAR

Once you've passed the hurdles of connecting the phone, and of teaching drivers how to activate the voice recognition system, you still have to tackle the design.

Here's a sample of an earlier version of Ford SYNC's music system (see Figure 8-10). Rather than Bluetooth, users needed to plug the phone or music player in via a wire and the USB port. Also, every time users wanted to speak, they first needed to press the Voice button on the steering wheel.

USER
[presses Voice button on steering wheel]

SYNC
SYNC. Please say a command.

USER
USB.

SYNC
USB. Please say a command.

USER
Uh, Bruce Springsteen?

SYNC

[harsh "boop boop" sound to indicate it did not understand]
You can request to play an album, artist, genre, track, or playlist. To
control media, say 'play,' 'pause,' 'previous track,' 'next track,' 'previous
folder,' or 'next folder.'

By reading that, it might not seem so bad. But imagine the poor driver.
In addition to the standard cognitive load people experience when listening to audio, add in the cognitive load of actually driving. First,
the user has to remember the obscure "USB" command. Then, there
were *28* commands related to playing music available to the user when
given the prompt "Please say a command." Users don't stand a chance.
[Thanks to Karen Kaushansky for the example.]

FIGURE 8-10.
Ford SYNC Music example

Rather than allow users to do everything, you should instead focus on
the main things users are likely—and want—to do. Sure, it's nice to
be able to say, "Play smooth jazz," but is that the primary use case?
Interactions in the car should be as simple and easy to remember as
possible. Take advantage of common tasks by shortcutting the process. For example, Ford SYNC later introduced a traffic feature that
made it possible for drivers to get the traffic report for their drive home.
Teaching the user which voice commands would be needed to set this
up is a difficult task, not to mention the difficulty of recognition for
address entry. Instead, users log in to their Ford SYNC account online
and set up their destinations. That way, in the car, the user can use a
simple command such as "traffic to home" and get just what is needed.

Be careful with your audio design, as well. One car navigation app allowed other people who saw you driving to send a "hello" type notification. The chosen audio was a "beep beep" noise—very distracting when you're driving.

To get around the difficulties of building native in-car systems, one solution is to let the mobile phone do the heavy lifting. Apple's Car Play (Figure 8-11) and Android Auto are two examples of this.

FIGURE 8-11.
Apple Car Play

Car Play works by plugging your iPhone into the car via lightning cable. It then uses the familiar iPhone interface on the car's touch screen. You can also start voice commands by pressing a button on the steering wheel. Car Play doesn't let you do everything you could normally do on an iPhone, but it allows for apps that are helpful in the car, such as navigation and playing music.

Android Auto (Figure 8-12) also uses a wired connection to the car, via a micro-USB-to-USB cable.

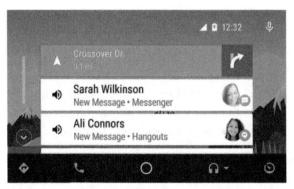

FIGURE 8-12.

Android Auto

Another advantage to using the phone rather than a built-in system is that the phone goes with you, so things you do in the car will be remembered later. For example, in the car you might want to set a reminder to pick up your dry cleaning; because you used the phone to create it, your phone can remind you later, regardless of where you are.

In addition, rather than forcing users to learn another complex set of commands, they are already familiar with talking to the phone.

DISTRACTED DRIVING

Now, even if you solve the recognition issues, and the user experience issues, there is one additional key factor that separates designing for the car from anything else: distracted driving. In 2015, the United States saw the highest one-year percentage increase in traffic deaths in half a century, according to the National Safety Council (NSC). Although some of this can be attributed to more drivers on the road, due to cheaper gas prices and economic improvements, some of it is due to the increase in distracted driving. According to the NSC, 26 percent of fatal car crashes are caused by distracted driving.[1]

As Lisa Falkson, lead voice UX designer at electric car company NextEV, points out, there are three types of driver distraction in the car: cognitive, visual, and manual. Texting while driving is at the nexus of all three.

Jared Strawderman, senior manager of user experience at electric car company Atieva, agrees that safety is crucial when designing VUIs for cars (emphasis mine):

---

1 "National Safety Council: Safety on the Road." (2015). Retrieved from *http://nsc.org/*.

Safety is just as big of a concern as usability when designing for cars. NHTSA guidelines specify that drivers should not look away from the road more than two seconds, which is likely too long in any case. Voice interfaces on mobile apps can defer to the screen when that is appropriate; by contrast, automotive VUIs do not have that luxury. Consequently, automotive VUI designers need to figure out a way to complete voice-initiated interactions without the screen as much as possible. **The key challenge when designing a voice interaction for the car is helping the user avoid the temptation of looking at their phone while driving.**

People are spending more and more time attached to their mobile devices. According to one small study at Baylor University, college students spend *nine hours* per day on their smartphones, 30 percent of which is spent texting.[2]

The promise of autonomous vehicles is on the horizon, but in the meantime, how do we enable people to do more in their cars without turning them into distracted drivers?

Speech recognition in the car is a bit like the earlier days of speech recognition on the phone: everything must be just right. Honda advises drivers "for best results, close all the windows, and turn down the climate control fan." Users must say their commands clearly and correctly, such as "Radio FM preset seven." A better design would do away with requiring the user to maintain such information, and simply say, "Play the radio station 97.3," or even better, "Play my favorite radio station."

Some cars display available voice commands on the screen when the user presses the talk button, which is highly distracting. And, although dictating a text message hands-free is arguably safer than looking down at your phone, it still adds distraction.

Other things that can reduce driver distraction include context-awareness. This can include things such as automatically pausing audio when a phone call comes in, saving the driver from frantically tapping their device. A great example of context-awareness comes from Cortana, which detects if your Bluetooth headset is on, and when a

---

2   "Cellphone Addiction Is 'An Increasingly Realistic Possibility,' Baylor Study of College Students Reveals.) (2014). Retrieved from *http://www.baylor.edu/*.

text message comes in while you're driving, announces who the text is from, and offers to play it out loud. It also offers the chance to respond. Here's an example of the Cortana experience for a user who is driving in the car. Again, the user must press the Talk button on the steering wheel before giving the voice command.

CORTANA
[pauses music] You got a text from Cathy. Wanna read it, or ignore it?

USER
Read it.

CORTANA
The message is: "I'm running late. Home by seven." Reply, call back, or are you done?

USER
Reply.

CORTANA
OK. What would you like to say?

USER
"That's fine, see you then."

CORTANA
OK. Texting Cathy, "That's fine. See you then." Send it, add more, or try again?

USER
Send it.

CORTANA
I sent your message. *[resumes music]*

This interaction allows the user to complete their task with no visual feedback. It also simplifies the commands so that Cortana can let the user know what's available at every state, without an overwhelming list of options. You can imagine an engineer somewhere saying, "But what if I only want to correct the word in the middle?" and getting fancy editing commands, but considering how short text messages are, there's no point. In addition, the responses from Cortana are very short. It's cumbersome to say, "Here is your message: <message>. Now, I can send that for you, or you can add more. Or, if it's wrong, you can try again. What would you like to do?" Instead, keep it short and sweet. Brevity is important in these situations.

TeleLingo's LingoFit has a dual approach to VUI in the car. Part of its mission is to alert drivers when they are distracted or drowsy. When LingoFit detects a driver is on "safe, traffic-free stretches of road, when the driver's attention exceeds the required level, LingoFit offers mind fitness exercises."

For example, LingoFit helps people prepare for upcoming presentations by asking questions about their slide content. It also offers assistance learning a foreign language. One of the advantages to being in the car is that it can use context; for example, if the driver is crossing a bridge, it can take the opportunity to teach the word "bridge" for better retention.

Strawderman also points out another difference between designing for mobile and car:

> Another factor is the relationship between the device and the user. For mobile devices, it's easy to establish who the user is by way of their ownership of the device. In other words, most mobile devices usually are not shared, whereas cars are often shared. This makes personalized experiences a bit more difficult, but not impossible.

In addition:

> But in a car, there are some critical use cases that require a visual affordance. For example, one of the obvious features frequently used in the car is the navigation system. When trying to convey details around traffic, alternate routes, point of interest result sets, and so on, you need an automotive UI with a screen. This is something that Echo users would likely have no expectation in getting from Alexa.

DEVICE SHIFTING

As mentioned earlier, as a designer, it's crucial to make the user's experience between being in the car and out of the car as seamless as possible. It's also vital to handle the case when multiple devices in the car are listening, such as the car, the phone, and a watch. Which one should listen? As Karen Kaushanksy said, "The one that can provide the best results based on context." She goes on to say, "Actually I don't care who listens...just do the right thing." Let all the devices listen, and "negotiate between them who answers." It can also be useful to let the user specify the device when needed, such as, "Save this to my watch."

If I'm driving and I ask, "Who won the Giants game last night?" my watch should detect I'm driving, and not display it. Instead, it could tell me the information out loud, or if the watch is not capable, ask the phone to do it.

Strawderman, who also worked on the Amazon Echo, appreciates the feature that allows you to device shift when listening to an audio book:

> I love how you can listen to a book on Audible on your mobile device through Bluetooth in your car, and walk into your house and Alexa knows exactly where you left off. That's a magical experience.

INTERACTION MODE

Choosing an interaction mode in the car is an important design decision. Will you require users to push a physical button before speaking? Will you require them to push the button only the first time, but be able to respond within one conversation without doing so? What about using a wake word?

So far, push-to-talk has been the dominant model. It's a very practical decision because it means the car does not need to constantly listen to see if the user is speaking to it. Another advantage is that push-to-talk can automatically mute or dampen any audio, such as music or a podcast, to improve recognition accuracy. Finally, unlike with a device such as the Echo, you know where the driver will be: in a car. The driver will be close to the button on the steering wheel at all times, not across the room and sitting on the couch.

On the other hand, as devices such as Amazon Echo and Google Home become more common, people might grow more accustomed to that model and expect similar behavior in their cars. The ideal approach might be a hybrid: push-to-talk to initiate a new conversation, but allow users to respond without it while within the conversation. For example, in the earlier Cortana text message scenario, when Cortana asks, "Would you like to hear it, or ignore it?" it could listen for the user's response for a short window, with no button. Or if the user pushes the button to select a song but it's ambiguous ("Did you want to hear 'I Kissed a Girl' by Katy Perry, or by Jill Sobule?"), allow the user to say "Jill Sobule" without pushing it again.

CONCLUSIONS ON CARS

It can be enticing to design VUI experiences that allow drivers to use all of their mobile phone features, but be cautious. People do want to do a lot of things in the car, but that doesn't mean designers should let them. One of the reasons it's often less distracting to speak to someone in the passenger seat than someone on the phone is that the passenger is situationally aware and stops talking when the driver is engaged in a trickier driving situation, such as maneuvering around an object in the roadway. Someone on the phone, or your VUI, doesn't know when the driver needs to concentrate more. Focus on the most common and useful tasks, and design them in a simple, straightforward way to minimize driver distraction and keep us all safe on the road.

In the not-too-distant future, autonomous vehicles will become available, and designing VUIs for the car will enter an entirely new phase. Driver distraction will no longer be an issue, but new things will arise, such as privacy when ride-sharing. It might be that speech is not always the best mode; perhaps a passenger would prefer to press a button to roll down the window rather than voice a command.

Strawderman also brings up the challenge of trust:

> The problem I see with voice in the car today is a profound lack of trust among users. VUIs in the car are still primarily command-and-control type interactions and fall apart pretty quickly if the user doesn't say exactly what the system is expecting. As automotive original equipment manufacturers become brave enough to do NLU right and support enough meaningful functionality behind it, users will gain trust. When we get to a point where users can say anything to their cars the way they do their phones and have the confidence that they'll hear a useful response most of the time, voice will become a more prolific way for users to interact while in the car.

Special thanks to Jared Strawderman, Lisa Falkson, and Karen Kaushansky for their assistance with this section.

Conclusion

VUIs aren't just for phones anymore. They're expanding to the car, your wrist, and even your refrigerator. Devices have their own design challenges that can differ from an IVR or mobile experience.

As of this writing, many new devices and car VUIs are arriving in the near future. As they become more common, it's important not to lose sight of the goal: making them enjoyable and easy to use.

[*Epilogue*]

VUIs have come a long way since their 1950s inception. The VUIs of today are more similar to science-fiction dreams than ever. With just my voice, I can request a song (from a list of millions), order a car to come pick me up, find out the population of Uzbekistan, or send a message to someone thousands of miles away.

VUIs have not caught on everywhere yet, but their popularity is growing. A recent *Business Insider* article estimates that 504 million people will have used digital assistants, and projects by 2021 that number will grow to 1.8 *billion*.[1] Many of these interactions are already via voice, and as natural-language understanding technology improves, no doubt more of those actions, especially those in your home, will be voice-driven.

Recently, I called my dad to wish him happy birthday. We asked our Amazon Echo to sing happy birthday, and the four of us—myself, my husband, our son, and Alexa—sang together. Alexa is becoming a trusted member of our household that we speak to every day. When my son asked us how to spell a word while doing his homework and we didn't tell him, he said, "Fine, I'll just ask Alexa!" When I had to reboot my router and wanted to see if the Echo was connected, I spontaneously asked, "Alexa, are you working?" She replied, "Everything seems to be working." How much better is that than looking at flashing lights or a graph on my smartphone?

---

1   Dunn, J. (2016). "Virtual Assistants Like Siri and Alexa Look Poised to Explode." Retrieved from *http://businessinsider.com/*.

Right now, home assistants like the Echo and Google Home are fun gadgets. They are luxuries that might even seem like frivolous toys. But there is a reason that movies like *2001: A Space Odyssey*, *Star Trek*, and *Her* use VUIs as important parts of the story: it's seamless communication with computers. Humanity yearns to communicate. When no one's around, we talk to our pets and our TVs. We want to talk to our computers, too. Until recently it has not been a real possibility. And we still have a long way to go. But with the right design principles, VUIs don't need to be a simple gimmick. They can fundamentally change the way we interact with technology, making it so that we have to act less like computers, and more like people.

[*Products Mentioned in This Book*]

MOBILE PHONE ASSISTANTS

- Assistant.ai
- Cortana
- Hound
- Ok Google
- Robin
- Siri

HOME ASSISTANTS

- Amazon Echo
- Athom's Homey
- Google Home
- Ivee
- Mycroft

TOYS/OTHER

- Eagle Eye Freefall, Telefon Projekt
- Hello Barbie (Mattel and ToyTalk/PullString)
- Jibo
- Sophia by Hanson Robotics
- ThinkGeek's *Star Trek* "Com Badge" (*http://www.thinkgeek.com/ product/jmgi/*)
- You Don't Know Jack

APPS

- Gracie avatar (SILVIA)
- Merly
- Moodies (Beyond Verbal)
- Sensely
- SpeakaZoo (ToyTalk)
- Volio (including Talk to Esquire)
- The Winston Show (ToyTalk)

VIDEO GAMES

- *Binary Domain*
- *There Came an Echo*
- *Verbis Virtus*

WATCHES / BANDS

- Apple Watch (*http://www.apple.com/apple-watch-series-1/*)
- Microsoft Band (*http://bit.ly/2g5rkO2/*)
- Moto 360 (*http://amzn.to/2eNJvm4/*)
- Pebble (*http://amzn.to/2f32n1b/*)

CARS

- 2016 Honda Odyssey (*http://bit.ly/2eNOUto/*)
- 2009 Ford SYNC music example (*http://bit.ly/2eNN8IB/*)
- Apple Car Play (*http://www.apple.com/ios/carplay/*)
- Android Auto (*https://www.android.com/auto/*)
- LingoFit (*https://www.youtube.com/watch?v=-9Fs0PrGFKE*)

[*Index*]

About the Author

Cathy Pearl is Director of User Experience for Sensely, where she helps to bring their virtual nurse avatar to life, making her conversational and empathetic when talking to patients with chronic health conditions.

Cathy has been interested in talking to computers since she was a child and wrote her first conversational program on the Commodore 64. She studied cognitive science and computer science and learned about psychology, linguistics, human–computer interaction, and artificial intelligence. She has been designing voice user interfaces since 1999, when she started at Nuance Communications. She has worked on everything from helicopter pilot simulators at NASA to a conversational iPad app that has *Esquire* magazine's style columnist tell the user what they should wear on a first date. During her time at Nuance and Microsoft, she designed voice user interfaces for banks, airlines, healthcare companies, and Ford SYNC.

Colophon

The animal on the cover of *Designing Voice User Interfaces* is a blue-headed Pionus parrot (*Pionus menstruus*). This bird inhabits forest canopies throughout tropical South America and southern Central America.

In addition to the blue head and neck for which it is named, the Pionus sports green, iridescent plumage and red feathers under its tail. Most of these parrots grow to about 11 inches long.

Pionus parrots are not particularly talkative, but prone to making high-pitched screeching calls. Still, they are considered to be calm and quiet compared to other parrot species. Highly intelligent and sociable, they make popular pets. While its lifespan averages 35 years, some survive as long as 60 years.

Many of the animals on O'Reilly covers are endangered; all of them are important to the world. To learn more about how you can help, go to *animals.oreilly.com*.

The cover image is an animal illustration by Karen Montgomery, based on a vintage image (loose plate, source unknown). The cover fonts are URW Typewriter and Guardian Sans. The text font is Scala Regular; and the heading font is Gotham Narrow Medium.

Learn from experts.
Find the answers you need.

Sign up for a **10-day free trial** to get **unlimited access** to all of the content on Safari, including Learning Paths, interactive tutorials, and curated playlists that draw from thousands of ebooks and training videos on a wide range of topics, including data, design, DevOps, management, business—and much more.

Start your free trial at:
oreilly.com/safari

(No credit card required.)

CPSIA information can be obtained
at www.ICGtesting.com
Printed in the USA
LVOW05s2114301117
558158LV00007B/59/P